A GE Case Study:
The Self-Directed Work Team

LETTING GO

A GE Case Study:
The Self-Directed Work Team

LETTING GO

Cost-based productivity soared 106%
when management loosened the reins at
the GE Business Information Center

by

James R. Burnside

High Peaks
Press

International Standard Book Number: 0-9624923-1-0

Library of Congress Catalog Card Number: 92-73013

High Peaks Press
2307 Cayuga Road
Schenectady, New York 12309

Printed in the United States of America

DEDICATION

■

This book is dedicated to a small group
of GE people who have successfully begun
a journey to address a major problem facing
corporate America in the '90s— raising
productivity and lowering costs without
sacrificing quality or customer satisfaction.

CONTENTS

∎

FOREWORD

■

Toward the end of 1990, representatives from Ford, 3M, Honeywell, and other major businesses began to come to Albany, New York, to investigate a GE organization which they had heard was a benchmark for new customer service centers. The organization was the GE Business Information Center (GEBIC).

A typical reaction from one of the visiting executives: "I find this hard to believe."

What they found was a series of paradoxes.

First, there was indisputable evidence of a sharp, continuing increase in productivity at GEBIC. Over a three-year period, it rose 106% while cost per customer served dropped 46%. Concurrently, customer satisfaction climbed sharply. Today, two thirds of customers surveyed rate GEBIC perfect on a scale of one to 10. Less than one per cent express any problem.

Second, the visitors were impressed by the employees who, individually and as a group, gave the impression they were in charge. But, in the same breath, the employees spoke highly of their manager. In another paradox, the manager's role in managing had actually diminished over the past year; his prime concern had been to transfer ownership of the business to the employees.

And, finally, the GE component which had been transformed—the GE Business Information Center—was a *service* business, where in the past most gains in this kind of team-building had been made in manufacturing.

The transformation began in 1989 when management decided that GEBIC should become a self-directed work team. But merely saying so, of course, was not enough.

First, management had to commit to the concept of "letting go"—to transfer in fact as well as theory both power and responsibility from managers to employees. Then, both groups had to commit to the considerable time and energy needed to effect the change.

GEBIC was responding to CEO Jack Welch's call for GE businesses to become lean and agile in the face of intense worldwide competition—what Stephen Roach of Morgan Stanley has called "the great equalizer."

During the early years of the '80s, GE productivity grew by one to two per cent a year. By 1991, the rate had climbed to six per cent. That growth is a crucial priority for GE: each point of productivity improvement produces $350 million of pre-tax income.

A successful GE response, says Welch, will engender an entrepreneurial change that competitors will find hard to match. "Corporate Gullivers," he predicts—whether them or us—"are doomed without speed, simplicity and self-confidence."

Easy to say. But a tall order to fill. What the CEO is really asking for is the hardest of all corporate tasks—changing the *culture* of a business, or even a corporation.

The chairman's challenge actually represents more of a strengthening of GE tradition than the abrupt departure it seems to suggest. Since the company was founded by Thomas Edison more than a century ago, GE has nudged outward the frontiers of research as its people strove to develop new and better products and, equally important, new and better styles of management.

The move to self-direction doesn't imply that the old styles of management were bad. Rather, it's a recognition that while the old methods were fine for their times, they don't work very well in today's business world. The world has changed, and it's time for management styles to change, too.

At first, the people of GEBIC—like others who have entered the labyrinth of self-direction—found it difficult to cut a clear path. What finally evolved from their struggle was a simple, six-step process:

1. *Getting to Know You.*
2. *Setting Sights.*
3. *Sharpening Skills.*

4. *Taking Stock.*
5. *Unleashing the Power of Empowerment.*
6. *Getting Out of the Way.*

This case study detailing the steps taken by GEBIC is not another theoretical "how to" book that has a pat answer for everyone. Rather, it is a recounting of what happened to real people in a real-life business situation, in a company that is striving to strengthen its worldwide position of leadership.

The case study is presented in the hope that other businesses may benefit from GEBIC's experiences.

Those who do make the journey will find that the sights along the way are rich and rewarding and that, as GEBIC found out, the process works.

How This Book Came to be Written
■

The people of GEBIC asked me to document the story of their evolution because I had previously been a communications manager in what is now their parent organization, Corporate Marketing and Sales, and had a feel for their place in the GE universe.

My earlier contacts at GEBIC did not prepare me for the changes that had taken place since I left GE a few years back. Then, all of my dealings with GEBIC had been limited to the manager. Not anymore.

GEBIC's current manager, John Wilfore, had called me to get started on the book project and gave me an introductory briefing. But in short order the rest of the people of GEBIC immersed me in every phase of the business. They also applied to the book project most of the initiatives which I discovered later had been learned on their journey toward self-direction.

GEBIC members held a session to retrace for me the footprints of the six long steps they had taken. Others recreated their often roisterous meetings which kept hoisting higher their level of skills and productive procedures, at the same time melding their diverse talents into an integrated work team.

Over a period of several months, I interviewed every member at length, sat in with them as they went about their work, and talked with outsiders who had interacted with them. Up until this point, I had known only the external dimensions of GEBIC. This gave me the rare opportunity to probe for its soul.

When I finished the first draft, the people of GEBIC read the entire manuscript, then helped me edit, correct and repair it. Initially, the book ended with Chapter IX.

But they objected: "You can't stop there. Readers will ask, 'So what?' and we've got to give them an answer."

They were right, of course. So Chapter X was added, entitled 'Lessons Learned.' The lessons, as you might expect, were provided by the people of GEBIC.

"Letting Go", therefore, is mostly the joint product of the individuals shown on the cover. Throughout, in both their words and actions, they underscore the book's major conclusion: the operative word in self-direction is "Go."

J.R.B.

The Challenge
■

John F. Wilfore, a GE manager who had been with the company for 28 years, felt a growing uneasiness as he left corporate headquarters in Fairfield, Connecticut, in early July 1989 and headed for home on the New York State Taconic Parkway.

His unease stemmed from mixed emotions.

On the one hand, Wilfore was buoyed by good news. He had just been promoted to head the GE Business Information Center in Albany, New York, which had been established in 1984 to help business-to-business customers find order in a complex company. Before that, industrial callers not served regularly by GE sales representatives were often ferried from office to office within the company in the hope that somewhere, somehow, someone might offer safe harbor.

GEBIC, therefore, had been put in place to provide a telephone linkage for callers to someone in GE who cared and who could help.

Along with the heady news of Wilfore's promotion, however, came the downside: he had been handed, as a fait accompli, the mandate to "delayer." This was a euphemism for slimming down reporting levels of management.

At the time, GEBIC was organized in the hierarchical form that is still typical of most U.S. companies. There was a section manager with over-all responsibility; three sub-section managers who split the responsibility for operations, market information and systems; and 17 other employees. The latter were divided into two functional groups— program directors, who handled the incoming calls, and the remaining people who took care of internal support activities.

John Wilfore had been one of the three sub-section managers. Delayering meant that this entire secondary level of GEBIC sub-section managers would now be eliminated. Wilfore knew that it also meant he would have to help relocate or reassign his two former peers, both long-time colleagues and friends.

While this was a culture shock in itself, he was perplexed even more by a new challenge that came along with the assignment: he was told to transform GEBIC into a self-directed work force.

Wilfore's concern sprang from a natural source—the unknown. Before leaving Fairfield, he had asked a few people what self-direction was all about, and they gave him the same answer: "We don't know."

The term itself conjures up disaster scenarios:

- Self-direction, by definition, means giving away power to the employees. What role is left for the manager?

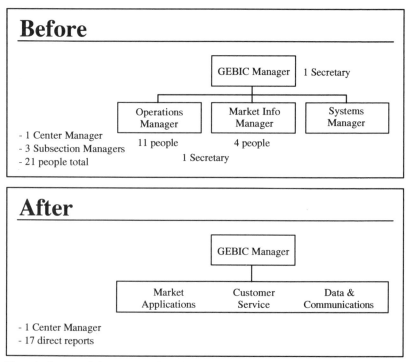

The challenge of delayering. GEBIC's newly appointed manager is given the charter to transform his new "flat" organization into a self-directed work team.

- With delayering the peer relationship among managers would dry up. Isn't it bad business for the boss to get too chummy with employees?
- Delayering also means there will be fewer chances for promotion. What does the manager do when 'the natives are restless?'
- The traditional task of management has been to decide what employees learn and do. Does that get pushed to the wayside by self-direction?

Wilfore was sure that other GE managers would have to wrestle with these same questions. But he was not nearly so sure that he or any of the others knew the answers to many of the questions that were yet to be asked.

John Wilfore's new boss was Richard Costello, the head of GE Corporate Marketing Communications. Before John had left Fairfield, Costello reiterated the role he wanted John to fulfill as the new manager of GEBIC, and re-emphasized why the service center had been assigned to his corporate component.

"As you know," Costello told John, "GEBIC serves as the company's front door for unserved customers and prospects. Therefore, it's important that your people emulate what's instinctive to every good sales person: *listen* to the customer to find out how to serve him or her better. In GEBIC's case, this means that your program directors should satisfy customers when they first call or, if they can't, they should refer them to GE experts around the company who have the right answers."

When GEBIC does a good job of directing inquiries to the GE sales forces, continued Costello, it's bound to burnish the company's image. "That's why GEBIC was placed in GE Corporate Marketing and Sales. It's in support of GE people all over the company."

Costello told Wilfore that he could provide no roadmap that would lead John and his people to self-direction. But he did outline the theory of the case, as envisioned by Jack Welch, that would point them in the right direction:

Cut out the layers between management and the troops, and you accomplish two key things—you get rid of much non-productive "work", and open up clear channels for complete and continual two-way communications.

The latter process, in effect, replaces old-style GE strategic *planning*, which not only documented goals but spelled out how to achieve them in infinite detail. The new concept is more properly called strategic *intent*.

In simplest terms, the manager becomes a leader, or coach, rather than a manager. He or she helps people determine *what* to do, but not *how* to do it. The manager helps them get the necessary skills, learns some new skills of his own, empowers his fellow workers, then gets out of the way.

Costello readily admitted to Wilfore that he didn't know how to build a self-directed work team. But, he affirmed, "I'm committed to make the process work, and will provide the needed resources."

Costello also made it clear to John that he wanted to participate and be a part of the process. "I want to make the trip with you and your people."

As John Wilfore continued driving along the parkway, he mused at the dimensions of this management challenge.

The manager's role in the self-direction process, John Wilfore learns, is different than it is in a traditional business organization. The manager is expected to *lead*, not *manage*.

In one way, his uneasiness was tinged with confidence. He knew he was not alone among GE managers. He also knew that upper management would send along if not assurance, at least support and understanding as he and the others trudged up the learning curve.

Nor did the new challenge fall outside of the traditional pattern most GE managers were long used to facing. On starting out, there usually was no clear-cut focus on what was to be done or where to turn for help. As his old job description stated, it was just one more "opportunity to grow" while one learned and solved problems.

In addition, Wilfore was reassured by the thought that upper GE management wouldn't have handed him the challenge of self-direction if they hadn't felt he was up to the task.

To some GE managers of Wilfore's time span, inured for so long from change, the organizational restructuring going on in GE was a recipe for anarchy. Delayering, for example, meant that section managers would lose the venerable management filter they had always had. In Wilfore's case, he now would have a "flat" organization with a large span of control— 17 direct reports.

It likely meant that John would have to come to grips with the kind of turbulent future unfolded by business guru Tom Peters. It was a great time to be alive if you didn't mind "Thriving on Chaos."

The invitation extended by GE to its employees seemed to say: come along while we build a better company, get more satisfaction out of what you do, and enjoy the sights along the way.

So GEBIC's new manager, John Wilfore, turned off the parkway, which he had traversed so many times before, to begin a new venture into uncharted territory.

Without a map.

He was game to give it a try, and he hoped the people of GEBIC would be, too.

Whatever happened, it promised to be an exhilarating journey.

Step One:
Getting to Know You
■

Employees who are invited to participate in a business program can usually tell how good it's going to be by the reaction to the kick-off meeting.

Most of the those who filed out of the GEBIC conference room in Albany when Richard Costello announced the new program in mid-July 1989 must have felt that theirs was doomed to disaster. Most of them had no idea what he was talking about.

In fact, as Costello and John Wilfore admitted later, neither of them really understood the consequences of the journey they were about to undertake.

The fact that Costello was there told the attendees the meeting was important. As head of GE Corporate Marketing Communications, Costello was responsible not only for GEBIC but for GE's brand image ("We bring good things to life") beamed to the company's millions of customers and prospects. He was also in charge of GE's Horizons pavilion in Epcot Center at Walt Disney World in Orlando, Florida.

It was a good bet that Costello would not kick off a meeting of 18 people in upstate New York if he did not have a high priority agenda and did not intend to fully support the program.

Wilfore had sensed that the outcome of this meeting would set the course of his future career at GE. While the proposition was intriguing, it was unlike anything he had ever encountered in the company. Along with his new job, he had been asked to achieve a goal that was ill-defined— not only had the term "self-directed" not been explained to him, it was not even in the dictionary.

Wilfore had devoted almost half of his GE career to marketing and communications management. His orientation had been shaped by a GE management style lauded by the business world since the '50s. As a result of that schooling, Wilfore—like his GE compatriots in the '80s—was task-oriented and initiated work based upon definable goals.

This was why, as his first move after becoming GEBIC's manager, he had decided to ask Costello to attend their kick-off meeting, put the goal on the table, and solicit ideas for the task. After all, John concluded, "self-directed" implied that others should share some of his new challenges.

Or, maybe the meeting would just get things moving in the spirit of Woody Allen, who opined that "90% of life is just showing up."

Even showing up suggested trouble to Brian Babe, a GEBIC program director at the time. "Back then," he observed, "a GE general manager never called a special meeting unless there was a problem."

Costello did lay out one problem at the meeting: "I'm sorry to report that all of the current GEBIC managers except one will be leaving. They're in the process of relocating to new positions in GE." Then he added with a smile, "I'm pleased to tell you that the one who will stay at GEBIC is John Wilfore. He's your new manager."

After a few pleasantries, Costello switched to the meat of the meeting. "As you know, Jack Welch is convinced that the only way we're going to keep our lead over foreign competitors nipping at our heels is for GE to become more productive and better at what we do.

"One of the early moves made by our new CEO was to restructure and get rid of layers of management. But," he cautioned, "there is more to come and don't think GEBIC is being picked on just because you're losing your sub-section managers. This winnowing began in the early '80s at the very top, where GE cut out both its Group Executives and Sector Vice Presidents. Delayering has helped streamline all of GE's businesses.

"So has automation," he continued. "But as Welch has pointed out, that doesn't do much when people just hide inefficient processes and unproductive work cultures by automating them. And it's no answer at all if you believe you can succeed without, or despite, your people. Of course, you can't."

People, said Costello, are the key issue at GE. And what does that mean for GEBIC?

"With fewer people and the elimination of your secondary management layer, we have the opportunity to find ways to become more efficient and to assume new duties and responsibilities. At the same time, we have to do a better job serving customers. The proposed method is to become a 'self-directed' work force. First, we have to figure out how to do that. There will probably be quite a few forks in the road that will take us there, but neither John nor I know where they are or which one will lead to where we want to go."

The eyes of his listeners glazed over at the terms he and Wilfore bandied about as they began to speculate about venturing into unknown territory: Empowerment. Open communications. Boundaryless business. Team-building. Work-Out.

The latter was an emerging company-wide program which Welch had announced late the previous year, in 1988. As yet, it was no more than words on paper for the troops in the GE outposts.

"I'd heard most of the terms used in the meeting," says Margi Call, GEBIC's Program Manager—Operations. "But they related more to stories about manufacturing in Japan. And open communications had always been lacking at GEBIC."

Like others who had been with GEBIC for some time, she posed to herself the traditional questions: "Who will be appointed to take over the functions of the departing managers? How will those of us still left be organized? And how will we be affected?"

Loretta Wilary, Program Manager—GEBIC Support, was puzzled by the new charter from Costello. She could not imagine such a fundamental change in the way GEBIC conducted its business. Her conclusion: "I didn't believe it was possible to get everyone to buy into this new team approach."

The others, reflecting their background and training, reacted to the program in different ways.

The newer people, while not understanding, were at least willing to listen. They hoped the proposed steps would lead them to firm ground from the shifting sands of inexperience.

In contrast, some of the more experienced employees were alarmed. Once more they felt the tremors which, throughout the '80s, had loosened the comfortable and familiar grip they had always felt they had on their jobs. Kevin Vaughn, who heard about it much later in the process after joining GEBIC as a program director, says he saw the same thing at his previous employer, the credit agency of a Fortune 500 firm. "When they tried self-direction, people saw it as a threat. As one cynic noted, 'It's giving the keys to the inmates.'"

In between were the bulk of the employees who foresaw the usual troubles in coping. How was the work going to change? What would it do to them personally?

Brian Babe was one of those who just didn't know. But his reaction was more visceral than vexing: "I think they're full of baloney."

In spite of the uncertainties that littered the road ahead, Richard Costello viewed the challenge of self-direction in a positive light. In fact, he felt the people of GEBIC had more to gain than lose.

Up until now, he reasoned, the GE Business Information Center had been working well, comparable in most respects to other customer service centers. If the new venture did not turn out successfully, GEBIC could always return to its old way of doing business.

The negative aspect, of course, was the risk of a precipitous drop in quality and productivity because of some unforeseen quirk in the process. There weren't many scouting parties with experienced guides on this new frontier.

But the process did offer the promise of improved performance and more satisfied customers. If this did come about, GEBIC would surely outperform its competitive peers.

The risk, Costello felt, was minimal. So his concluding words to the people of GEBIC at the kick-off meeting were: "Let's move ahead together."

To begin with, John Wilfore asked his co-workers to help him look for program guidance. The GE Work-Out program offered some promise, but a detailed implementation plan with specifics was still somewhere upstream. By the time it floated down, the people of GEBIC would have formulated their own objectives and launched programs to accomplish their own goals.

As their search got under way, they discovered that the shelves were full of periodicals and books on work teams, ranging from Freud to Maslow and from Abernathy to Yankelovich. Most explored scholarly concepts supported by case examples. The problem was that many skipped lightly over the "soft" service aspects of business to concentrate on the "hard" tangibles of manufacturing.

Wilfore and his people were soon befuddled by an overload of general information and frustrated by the lack of practical blueprints. At the same time, they were distracted by the day-to-day realities of running the business.

When Wilfore reported the dilemma to Costello, he replied, "What we need now is objectivity. Let's find somebody who can point us in the right direction and keep us lined up as we move on."

Julie Dinardo, who joined GEBIC as a program director when the search for help was getting under way in September 1989, shook her head at the prospect. "I had just come from a major oil company. It had the same management hierarchy that GE used to have, and was making the same kind of structural changes— closing plants, consolidating sales districts, and so on.

"The firm had targeted team-building as their second goal," said Julie. "When I left, most people were working in teams. But as far as I know, self-direction was never on their schedule.

"John told me that's where GEBIC was headed. It didn't take me long to think: 'Oh, oh— we're not even a team yet, let alone a self-directed team. We have a long, long way to go.' "

Bill Waers, at the time a manager for GE Appliances Telesales, suggested that GEBIC get in touch with a consultant whom Waers had worked with in the past— Gary

Martini, of Martini & Associates, Minneapolis, which specialized in organization and team development and training. To get things moving, GEBIC asked both Martini and an in-house GE consulting services team to make competitive presentations to GEBIC, spelling out details of their proposed programs.

The employees unanimously chose Martini. This first venture into the democratic process gave them a heady whiff of the promise to come from teamwork and self-direction.

While the give-and-take following Martini's presentation was, in effect, an interview by GEBIC of the consultant, he told Costello and Wilfore after the meeting that he was also interviewing them as *his* prospect. Martini said he looked forward to working with GEBIC for one major reason: "It was apparent to me that both Richard and John were serious about the venture and viewed it properly as an investment rather than a cost."

The people of GEBIC liked Gary Martini for more than his presentation. He had previously worked for 10 years in three of GE's major businesses— jet engines, lighting and appliances. Therefore, he didn't have to start from scratch in skirting the pitfalls of a shifting GE culture. On his visit to GEBIC, he demonstrated a melding of practical GE

A basic need: commitment. GEBIC's consultant, Gary Martini (center), assures himself that John Wilfore (left) and Richard Costello, Manager of GE Corporate Marketing Communications, are serious about their new venture and see it as an investment, rather than a cost.

experience with the consulting skills he had first forged at Case Western University in Ohio, and then honed and wielded in the field.

Gary also brought along a good supply of the two most valuable traits in business— common sense and a sense of humor. "You can measure my progress at GEBIC," he told them, "by how quickly I work myself out of a job."

To help GEBIC people gain perspective, Martini suggested they make on-site visits where self-directed teams were already in place: two AT&T operations— Transtech in Jacksonville, Florida and AT&T Credit in New Jersey; GE Appliances Telesales operation in Louisville, Kentucky; GE Lighting's National Customer Service Center in Richmond, Virginia; and a smooth-running operation conducted by the Aid Association for Lutherans at Appleton, Wisconsin.

The more they saw, the more they realized how different each operation was and how little they knew. Their consultant put the challenge in perspective: "You first need a fundamental set of skills."

These, he said, will come in a series of phased team-building sessions. "They vary according to the needs of an individual business. At GEBIC, we should start with team formation— exercises that show how groups evolve, behave and perform, followed by training with problem-solving tools."

Next should come sessions to create a "vision," or mission, for GEBIC. From this, we can extract long-range goals and form teams to handle tasks that address each goal, Martini outlined. The teams will then identify the obstacles and the intermediate objectives necessary to achieve the long-range goals.

Martini cautioned that team-building must be built upon a solid foundation. "The first step in its construction calls on us to learn more about ourselves and each other."

Mike Marchi, who was GEBIC's Manager of Market Information Applications at the time, remembers that "team-building sounded like a great idea to me. Gary had said, 'If you prepare people by building a strong team, then they can handle most problems. But if you start with the problem before people are ready with the necessary skills, you're asking for trouble.'

"The 'getting to know you' aspect was something else, however," adds Mike. "Most of us didn't know what to expect."

"I certainly didn't," says Julie Dinardo. "But being new to GEBIC, it sounded like a good way to meet people. And I looked forward to the first team-building sessions, since we had no formal team training at my previous job."

Nora Richter, a GEBIC senior program director, recalls her first reaction: "Is this for real, or just another GE program? But when Richard told us he would be there, I felt pretty sure he'd make things happen." Rosalind Wilkins, a GEBIC customer service representative, was intrigued because "I'd never been included in meetings before." So, she decided to "go with the flow and see what happens."

Gary Martini explained the underlying reason for the first session: each person is different and, therefore, not only has different strengths and abilities but different ways of perceiving and doing things. The mix is further complicated by people coming and going, and because members are always at different stages of development in the continuing process.

Understanding each other, he said, is crucial to team-building.

To underscore his commitment to the process, Costello scheduled the first session in November 1989 at the GE Horizons pavilion at Epcot Center in Orlando, Florida. Reactions were mixed. Some were thrilled by the journey— for one, it was a first airplane flight. Others arched eyebrows at the "fancy hotel." The caustic comment from one: "Why don't you just give us the money instead?"

Costello leveled the playing field by scheduling the Orlando session on the employees' own time over a weekend. After work on Friday, they flew to Orlando, attended sessions Saturday and Sunday, then flew back to Albany to begin work again Monday morning. Most of the follow-on sessions held at later dates in Albany were also held off-premise and again on employees' time.

This meshed perfectly with the consultant's view of the worth in involving everyone, at some sacrifice on their part for giving up their free time. They would come to recognize value in others' ideas, he believed, bolstered by time away from phones and the pressures of work and home.

GEBIC's session in Orlando was based upon the Life Orientations ®−(LIFO)−training concept developed by Dr. Stuart Atkins of Beverly Hills, and described in his book, "The Name of Your Game."
The session detailed the strength-based contrast between four distinct personality preferences as described by Dr. Atkins.

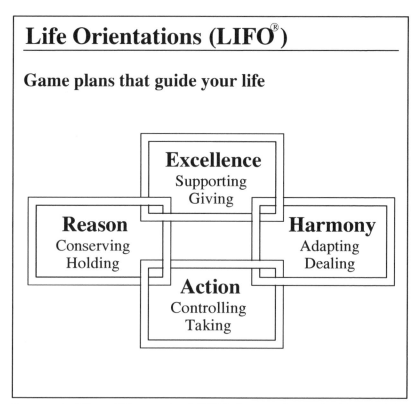

Life Orientations (LIFO®)

Game plans that guide your life

Excellence
Supporting
Giving

Reason
Conserving
Holding

Harmony
Adapting
Dealing

Action
Controlling
Taking

Everyone is different. The people of GEBIC discover that each of them exhibits a preference in at least one of these four personality life styles. During a Life Orientations (LIFO) session, they learn that their distinct differences actually strengthen their teamwork.

People in the first group are called Adapting/Dealing (AD)— they are people-oriented, and strive to work in harmony. Those in the second group, known as Supporting/Giving (SG), are characterized by excellence— they're perfectionists who aim for the very best in everything they do.

The third group is identified as Controlling/Taking (CT). Individuals in the group are the "movers and shakers"— dynamic, motivated to take quick action. And, finally, there is the Conserving/Holding group (CH)— they ask for the facts, and examine and evaluate alternatives in systematic, rational order.

Participants soon discovered that everyone showed strengths in each preference, but in varying degrees. Their conclusion: we're all different, and we all have a variety of strengths. And that's good.

The GEBIC people first identified their own preferences. Then, opposites paired up— usually, as then Senior Program Director Becky Raimo noted, "with someone you didn't know very well." They interviewed each other— about work, about their preferences, what made them what they are, their likes and dislikes, and so on. Afterwards, the pairs reported their findings to the assembled group.

In a burst of understanding, casual acquaintances from the office took on added dimensions of interest, warmth and emotion. "Before Orlando," says Becky, "we were your typical office: some people didn't know everybody or couldn't stand some of the others. But once we began to learn more about ourselves and one another, we got along just fine."

The gathering soon recognized that in almost every paired combination, the strengths of one co-worker complemented the strengths, or preferences, of the other. The consultant said that each person should "make the most of the hand you're dealt. Then, one can identify and fill in the missing perspectives."

The logical conclusion: GEBIC would not have the unique capabilities it did without the combined talents and strengths of all its people, with their unique and different LIFO styles.

Which led, for the first time, to an encouraging conclusion: GEBIC no longer viewed itself as just a collection of people. It was beginning to coalesce as a team.

"It was amazing to watch the process," says Richard Costello. "Here were people who had worked together for years and didn't know each other. The end of this first session gave me the first glimmer of promise that things were going to be different at GEBIC."

GEBIC people not only came to know and understand each other better, they began to form a clearer picture of their own roles, present and future.

The one whose role changed least was the consultant, Gary Martini. But the reason for his being there came into sharp focus for the attendees. As Senior Program Director Tom Lee notes, "it didn't take long to see how much we needed him. He was the catalyst that breathed life into our actions." Nora Richter agrees: "He was strong when he needed to be. He kept us focused, in spite of what we unknowingly did to sabotage the process."

Their comments confirmed what Martini had told them earlier, which no one paid much attention to: "There is a certain science to the process."

Costello was drawn to the project early on, Martini believes, by fascination as much as anything. In retrospect, Costello agrees. "I didn't understand it, but I asked them to count me in. I wanted very much to be part of the process."

And he did cover the major segments of the journey with the GEBIC crew. However, the presence of his rank was inescapable. At the Orlando meeting, for example, Costello was asked to welcome the attendees, but that was all. The team did not want him to get too involved ... at least not yet. His authority could have been intimidating.

"Perhaps his most valuable role," said Martini, "was to provide air cover during the entire process. He insulated them from many of the pressures that can disrupt a concentrated effort."

The first step taken by GEBIC at Orlando committed John Wilfore to a new course of business that was at odds with all the managerial moves he had observed and practiced over three decades. To some, the open mind it required exposed a traditional manager like him to great risk. "I would not have wanted to be in his shoes in those early days," says Julie Dinardo.

But Wilfore's learning curve veered upward. Gary Martini observes that John learned well the concepts stressed at Orlando.

David Cairns, a Program Director who joined GEBIC more than a year after Orlando, confirms it. "When I first arrived, John prepped me with a mini-LIFO session at our home base in Albany. Now, when I talk with others about the concepts John taught me, it's almost as if I had been at the Florida meeting."

Most GEBIC people welcomed the move that promoted a more open environment. "It made so much sense to break down the symbolic barriers that had been put up over the years," says Margi Call.

"Before," GEBIC Program Director Linda McClain observes, "I'm told everything was hush-hush, and it wasn't a very fun place to work. I'm sure the Orlando session started people talking and sharing."

The team-building initiated by this first step did not mean that every person carved out a comfortable, new niche at GEBIC. An employee report in the spring of 1991 noted that "many could not or did not want to adapt." As Tom Lee said, "some people are cut out to be individual contributors, not team players. Often, they'll 'blow smoke' for a while as a cover-up, make it look like they've bought in, but eventually leave."

Even the departure was positive for most. The budding GEBIC process helped define a new role for them elsewhere. Brian Babe was one of them.

Brian had always pegged sales as his career goal. He had been buoyed up on first coming to GEBIC because it offered him a bird's eye view of the total GE marketplace. Before long, he began to realize that being on the phone did not provide the face-to-face contact with customers that for him was the fulfillment of selling.

"I know the process that's underway at GEBIC is the trend in industry today, and I'm convinced GEBIC is trying to do the right thing. But being stuck on a phone just wasn't right for me." Shortly thereafter, Brian left to become a successful sales manager for GE Medical Systems in Toledo, Ohio.

The people of GEBIC had begun to learn only a few of the clues to team-building and self-direction in this first phase of their program. But they did gain a better understanding of certain fundamental principles.

First, they learned that team-building is like life — it's a journey and not a destination. Second, they learned that, as Marie Murray noted, "It's O.K. to be different" . . . that diversity is the unique ingredient which can imbue GEBIC with creative vitality, as it does to the diversified country that is the United States.

And finally, they came to appreciate the power of understanding— of 'getting to know you.' "We learned," says John Wilfore, "how quickly you can resolve issues if you just talk to one another."

The journey for GEBIC had begun.

Step Two:
Setting Sights
■

From the beginning of the process, Richard Costello and John Wilfore knew that they would have to think their way carefully through the thicket surrounding self-direction. They would have to first find not only a path that would lead GEBIC to it, but the right place to start.

Costello realized early on that he could provide no more than a general heading because there were no ready answers to many of the questions about the self-directed work force. He had therefore outlined the strategy for John in skeleton form only: tell your people what you want them to do, but not how to do it. Help them get some necessary skills. Learn some new ones of your own. Empower your fellow workers. Then get out of the way.

Instinctively, Costello knew that two more factors would have to be accommodated in the equation: aggressive action, and the interests of the customer.

Action, of course, reflected the energy which Jack Welch had injected into the "new" GE. In fact, much of his success as a CEO had come from two uncommon traits which were fueled by aggressive action.

One was a gut-level instinct that prompted Welch to cut through layers of inertia to reach the muscle where things happen— the do-it level. The other was a clear understanding that cultural change takes a long time and doesn't come from wallpapering over old habit patterns. As Welch said in a Harvard Business Review report in 1989, "This is a five-year process, probably closer to ten."

To both tasks, Welch brought the tenacity of a bulldog. He kept urging GE employees on with the interchangeable lures of change and opportunity, layering both with common-

sense suggestions on how to root out non-productive practices and share productive ones with co-workers.

Richard Costello felt comfortable marching to the
cadence of aggressive action. His style, by nature, was
no-nonsense and pragmatic. Over the years, he had
sharpened his skills aiming at the ultimate target of this
accelerating GE process— the customer.

He joined GE in 1980, coming from a worldwide advertising agency, McCann Erickson, to handle all marketing
communications for the company's $5 billion consumer
business. That customer base ballooned ten-fold when, in
1987, Corporate Marketing gave him responsibility for all
corporate aspects of GE customer communications, including not only advertising and promotion but direct marketing, telemarketing and exhibits.

The promise of self-direction for GEBIC would be ful-
filled, Costello reasoned, if John Wilfore and the GEBIC
team could respond positively to the interests of GE customers with the energy and minds of 18 people instead of
one faceless GE organization.

Wilfore concurred in the strategic concept of aggressive action. He had spent all his GE years in task-oriented
work, in technical and managerial positions concerning
customer service, marketing, sales, and computer-related
projects.

Wilfore's model for action had already been etched in
stone by Jack Welch. GE middle managers will be "the
stronghold of the organization," he had said. Each should
be "a combination of teacher, cheerleader, coach, and lib-
erator, not controller."

The guiding principle, said Welch, is to lead rather
than manage— to "create a vision, articulate the vision,
passionately own the vision, and relentlessly drive it
to completion."

What Welch was saying, in his own way, was that of
course every GE manager should take aggressive action.
But it still should be preceded by the "intolerable labor of
thought"— i.e., think before you act.

John's first challenge, then, before he could ask his people to swing into action, was to work with the team to

create a mission for the business—a mission that would focus and drive all employee actions.

Gary Martini proposed the mechanism for doing this: another off-site session, outside working hours, over the weekend at the local Holiday Inn. Martini said the session would be devoted to a concept which he had copyrighted called Strategic Visioning. It would, he said, help GEBIC "establish a guiding vision, long-range goals, and task teams."

But Martini caught their attention with another interesting paradox: "You can't do a vision."

The first thing you'll expect from visioning, he told them, is a glimpse of your future. "But visioning can never tell you what the future will be," he said. "All it can do is to visualize what you'd *like* the future to be. And to do that, you have to construct certain things in an orderly progression—a mission first, then goals, objectives, tasks and, of

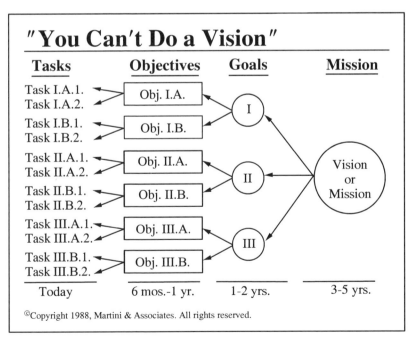

An interesting paradox. Visioning will never give you a glimpse of your future, warns Gary Martini. But it *can* help you visualize what you'd *like* it to be. It begins with a mission, which leads in an orderly progression towards goals, objectives and tasks.

course, teams to identify ways to accomplish the tasks and objectives that are necessary to achieve the desired long-range goals.

Costello and Wilfore looked forward to the session because it promised to move GEBIC one more step toward self-direction. Based upon their success at Orlando, John felt it should be smooth going. "Piece of cake," he thought.

"Close your eyes and think of yourself in a balloon which is about as close as you can get to outer space," Gary Martini told the gathering. "Now that you see the globe, close in on it until you see North America. Somewhere down there on the ground is a speck that's the GE Business Information Center. As we drift closer and closer to it, imagine that you can see the GEBIC of the future. Then ask yourself, 'what would you like things to be like five years from now?' First, think in a macro sense. Then, as we drift further down, think in micro terms of the specific things you'd like to see done at GEBIC."

Program Director Julie Dinardo remembers it as "an exhilarating exercise. Gary told us to let our minds go, and we did. Of course when you think about work, your thoughts drift back and forth into home life, too. That kind of thinking is really hard."

Richard Costello seconded that judgment. "It was one of the most intense sessions I've ever attended," he says. "You could almost see the wheels turn in people's heads as the day rolled on."

At first, many were reluctant to say what was on their minds. Then, slowly, participants began to toss out ideas to test for turbulence.

"Why should GEBIC remain domestic in scope?" asked one participant. "We can see the whole world from up in the balloon. Why don't we join the rest of the world or, at the very least, add someone on staff who can speak other languages?"

Nora Richter remembers it as "exciting, at times, but tiring, too. It's hard to get people in a group to agree on a common vision. There were people who had been with GEBIC a long time and others who were brand new, all with their own experiences. The session really brought out the personality differences."

Program Director Karen Malaczynski recalls that "we went in as 'them' and 'us' and tossed a lot of loud 'yes's' and 'no's' back and forth. But it got things out in the open, which we had never done before, and brought us together."

Gradually, random ideas gravitated toward key issues: What was GEBIC's central purpose? What core service should they provide? What kind of environment did they want to work in? And, finally, how should they work together?

The easiest question to answer was the first, concerning their primary goal, because it would surely relate to one of Costello's key points of leverage—the interests of the customer. The last question promised to be the most difficult, because while an obvious answer was teamwork, the give and take of participants during the day had exposed some wobbles in the course of the balloon.

Those wobbles threatened a violent turn in the flight path during dinner on the first night. As in any work environment, hidden factions began to surface with their hidden agendas.

The major tear in the GEBIC fabric divided those who maintained direct phone contact with customers—the program directors—from all the others—the support staff. It was a clear cut issue, recalls Rosalind Wilkins, who was a secretary at the time. "Some people felt they had control, while other people wanted control."

The volatile views steered the meeting on a collision course. Egos of the vocal expanded, while those who normally fell silent now declared they would *never* take a back seat in the new venture.

Some revealed long surpressed feelings: "You're the boss's favorite!" complained one. Said another, "You people up front work in a country club!"

For many, the real underlying question was: "What's in it for me?" For all, the questions revealed a lack of understanding and, therefore, a lack of commitment to each other and to the process leading to self-direction.

If nothing else, the after-dinner conversation identified areas of frustration and concern, as well as issues, that needed to be addressed. Since it was late, Gary Martini excused himself and retired for the evening.

"Gary didn't know it at the time," says Mike Marchi, "but it was as if he had pulled the pin on a grenade and rolled it on the floor as he left the room. There were some pretty hairy moments as we argued away into the night."

When the consultant convened the group in the morning, he sensed that many of their concerns were still unresolved. So he convinced them they should modify the agenda and again address the issues head-on. No progress could be made, he said, until the issues were resolved.

On perhaps the major one, the group came to realize that those who manned the phones in fact did need the help of the support people, and vice versa. There really was a strong dependency upon one another.

The contribution of the consultant, Costello discerned, "was group therapy. He showed us why we needed outside help. Without Martini," he continued, "I think it's likely we would have ducked the issue."

Most important, the group came to the grudging conclusion that to be successful, GEBIC had to operate as a team.

For the people of GEBIC, this represented a major milestone on their journey to construct a self-directed work force. It also represented a miraculous cleansing of the air. For the first time on their journey, they were able to gulp deep drafts of cooperation.

Martini cautioned them about one trap that many GE executives plunge into. Usually, he said, they are determined to nail on their goal post a specific measure of output, or a specific time for reaching a destination. In this case, he said, the journey itself is as important as the destination.

"Taking away the specifics made it a lot harder for us to put down our thoughts and goals," says Julie Dinardo. "In effect, he locked us in the room and made us define our mission— what we thought was important and what we wanted to do as a team.

"It's hard enough if you try to do it on your own," she continues. "But with 18 people, you tend to drown in semantics." To solve that problem, the group broke into four teams with each addressing a separate issue. They then reconvened and consolidated their findings.

"We struggled over every word," says Julie, "until we had the ones which defined exactly what we wanted to do. At the end, we were super proud of what we had accomplished." While it may not have been apparent to members of the group, it was their first real exercise in consensus, something that GEBIC would soon learn to live with on a daily basis.

If it had been a decade earlier at GE, GEBIC's task would have been to prepare a strategic plan. The manager would have defined long-range objectives and goals and a detailed analysis of external influences— competition, market trends, outlook for the economy, potential effects from pending legislation, resource allocations, etc., etc.

These would have been accompanied by proposed strategic thrusts, a tactical timetable, and step-by-step plans that told everyone in the organization what to do. The manager would then have sent it upstairs in draft form for

---

The GEBIC Mission

Each of us is dedicated to providing easy access to GE's commercial, industrial and technical products and services.

We, as a team of GE professionals, provide personalized attention and accurate answers.

We foster a dynamic and rewarding environment, built upon mutual respect and support.

We believe in sharing knowledge and the pursuit of continuous learning. Our bywords are adaptability, flexibility and team work.

"Committed to excellence, our customers and each other"

Compass heading. These five brief statements, defined by the people of GEBIC during an intense, soul-searching session, will now guide all their actions during their journey toward self-direction.

higher management to hone and strop until it had the right cutting edge and heft.

Only then would it have been revealed to those who would be responsible for carrying out the plans and reaching the goals— the work force.

Instead, what the people of GEBIC had done in a matter of a few hours was to put down, in four succinct sentences, a mission statement that was to guide the business and themselves in everything they were to do in the foreseeable future. The statement did not tell them *how* they were to do things. Rather, it defined more precisely *where* they wanted to be. The long-range goals and intermediate objectives told them *what* needed to be done.

The GEBIC staff did not realize it at the time, but with their mission statement they had cemented in place the keystone above the doorway that led to the self-directed work force.

As Costello started the car for his return trip to Fairfield after the turbulent, two-day session had ended, Wilfore added to his goodbye: "I'm glad you spent this time with us. Why should I have all this 'fun' by myself?"

Intuitively, the group had directed each statement of their mission at the key issues identified during the previous day. Once the words were down on paper, it became apparent that each statement had in reality defined a major goal for GEBIC. In short order, the group realized that each goal also called for a team which could focus and drive toward a solution.

The first statement in GEBIC's new mission addressed the members' point of leverage— the interests of the customer: "Each of us is dedicated to providing *easy access* to GE's commercial, industrial and technical products and services." There was no mistaking the goal, which the group underlined.

The second statement addressed the issue of GEBIC's core service: "We, as a team of GE professionals, provide personalized attention and *accurate answers*."

What kind of a workplace did they want at GEBIC? "We foster a *dynamic and rewarding environment*, built upon mutual respect and support."

And finally, how should the people at GEBIC work together? "We believe in *sharing knowledge* and the pursuit of continuous learning. Our bywords are adaptability, flexibility and teamwork."

Teamwork, in the military or a big corporation, is rarely voluntary. But the momentum of GEBIC's mission made team-building, as an outgrowth, almost an involuntary act. "No one hesitated to join in," remembers Mike Marchi. "Participation was 100%."

Viewpoints changed along with structure. "We had talked about teamwork before," says Margi Call, "but it was mostly just talk. In fact, our previous meetings had encouraged us to respect each other as individuals. But there had been no umbrella to bring us together, no natural way to find out what we had in common. Creating the mission along with the long-range goals and teams did the trick."

GEBIC veterans are still amazed that the teams formed so quickly and functioned so well, because there were neither assignments nor appointments. "Our consultant suggested we not have team leaders," says Tom Lee. "The object was to generate a healthy flow of ideas and make each of us feel and act like a leader."

Margi Call remembers that "those who were more talkative than others tended to take on lead roles, even though they had no more authority than the rest. We each tended to gravitate into roles we felt comfortable with.

"Flexibility made it work. We could take on a lead role if and when we wanted to, and if we thought we could do more good on another team, we simply moved over. It was," concluded Call, "and is, an invigorating experience."

Others noted the refreshing contrast at GEBIC from previous GE jobs. Loretta Wilary remembers that in years past as a secretary in an old-line GE business, "the work focus remained locked on a long-range business plan even though the market had changed drastically. Here, our mission hasn't changed, but our objectives and tasks change all the time."

Program Director Marie Murray recalls visioning as "the best part of the process. It forces you to have an action plan and to work toward the goals. If not, you tend to put things on the back burner."

The new team environment was the difference that lured Jacquie Braam from a customer service center in a GE product department to become a GEBIC program director. "My previous job had the same kind of set-up, with phones and Telex equipment, and I was in on a lot of decisions. But it wasn't the same as at GEBIC. There, we were on our own. Here, there's tremendous interaction between teams."

The word "commitment" is used so often in business that it tends to lose meaning. Even worse, it's not always supported on a foundation of fact.

The proper proof of commitment, GE people are fond of saying, is to "walk it before you talk it." GEBIC employees had not only stated their commitment to one another but began to take it out each day for a brisk jog in their pursuit of self-direction.

At this point, they knew they had made progress on their journey. But they felt frustrated because they could never be sure how far they had come or how much they had gained. For one thing, the composition of teams changed along with the changing interests of members; they were free to switch teams as they saw fit. Even worse, new hires lacked the orientation of those who had been through the earlier stages.

So the people of GEBIC decided to prepare an interim "trip" report that would satisfy a dual purpose. First, it would bring the new people up-to-date on what had already been done, and maybe gain some credit for GEBIC from others. And second, it would mold into finite shape the challenge that GEBIC saw for the future.

Ultimately, the document found its way to the GE executive office. Toward the end of the report was a brief page entitled: "Do you see what I see?"

It began: "Development of our mission signified the beginning or birth of our unified focus. What we are, where we are, and most importantly where we're going are embodied in the mission's few simple paragraphs.

"Each challenge we face as a group— the outcome, the way we handle it— can be measured against our mission. It keeps us on course, ensuring we are fulfilling our role, supporting each other, GEBIC, GE, and our customers."

Noble thoughts. But GEBIC people, like everyone else, knew they didn't work in a vacuum.

"New pressures— higher call volume that impacts on quality 10s (GEBIC's form of measurement), increased project work, presentations, plus personal pressures and problems— move our focus from 'what next?' to 'what now?' Our challenge is to maintain focus on our mission, continually thinking about 'what next?' and not to just focus on day-to-day. As we move toward uncharted paths together, who knows where we will go?"

Again, a noble expression of sentiments. But it begs the question: Does the process really work? Has it worked for the GE Business Information Center?

GEBIC formulated its mission in February 1990. Heeding the advice of its consultant, the group did not tie the mission to quantities or a timetable. But each team did establish measurable goals and target dates for achieving them— three to five years for major goals, one to two years for secondary objectives and programs.

In only a year and a half, the majority of the five-year goals had been accomplished. It was forceful testimony that their new mission had put GEBIC on a proper course— and that self-direction was working.

IV

Step Three:
Sharpening Skills
■

"Well, you've made it through basic training," Gary Martini told the GEBIC team members.

He recounted their accomplishments: "You've gotten to know each other, and to understand that each of you relies on the others. You've brought GEBIC's mission into focus. You've identified the goals to be achieved. And you've formed teams to work toward those goals."

But before you can proceed on your journey, said Martini, you need some new skills. He identified two milestones which GEBIC should strive for during this stage of the process.

The first was an understanding of group dynamics — skills that are essential in conducting effective meetings. And second, expertise in problem solving. These, he said, would serve as a jump-start to get GEBIC people up and running.

Martini also suggested that they should stop a good many times along their march to check for progress — to calibrate what was working, and what wasn't.

The word that they needed more training was nothing new to the people of GEBIC; GE had always stressed the importance of gaining new skills. But there were two new aspects. One was the focus on training for people who interact with the customer, and the other was the insistence that management learn the techniques of self-direction along with the employees.

GEBIC veterans groused about the need for more training. "We've done this time and time before, and nothing ever comes from it." But one young program director vowed, "it's up to us to see that the process *does* work."

In the true fashion of consultants, the first move Gary Martini made was — to call a meeting. "This is actually a meeting about meetings," he told them. "By analyzing group dynamics, you'll understand how groups evolve, behave and perform."

The consultant then led them on an exploratory tour of the nerve endings that play on meetings—factions, egos, tensions, conflicts, and so on. GEBIC members learned how to develop and hold to an agenda, recognize mounting problems, make course corrections through feedback and analysis, and so on.

Martini also introduced them to a brand new meeting participant—the process observer. "This adds the view of a dispassionate third party," he said. "This person, as the name implies, is not concerned with the content of the meeting, but with the meeting process. The process observer is a stabilizing factor in group dynamics."

GEBIC quickly recognized the value of the process observer. This individual ignores what's on the flipchart, and instead looks for signals from the nerve endings: Are people listening? Have they finished the topic? Has everyone's views been considered?

The process observer looks at the way things happen, records the methodology used, analyzes the "whys" of the actions, and then diagnoses ways to improve the process. Among the many roles of the process observer is that of a timekeeper and of a cheerleader.

The extra boost helps. David Cairns, who came to GEBIC more than a year after the group dynamics sessions were held, says, "It's amazing how you can put some 20 people with such different personality traits in the same room, and get so much done."

One reason, Paul Chmielewski believes, is that "people speak up more because they've learned they're not going to be shot down. We don't waste so much time now skirting the issues."

The second major area of skill building—problem solving—was a different matter. The people at GEBIC knew, of course, that every problem was different. But they discovered that almost any challenge could be simplified with the new techniques described by Martini.

One was storyboarding, which many GE operations use to analyze an issue and then construct a framework for action. Ideas generated on cards are tacked on the wall in columns that segregate the sub-points.

Tom Lee describes it as "an old fashioned brainstorming session, but it's visually oriented. There are a few rules— no put-downs, no evaluations . . . anything goes."

The evaluation comes after the storyboarding is complete, notes Tom. "But we always couple that with a commitment for action. For example, our need for a meeting handbook came out of a storyboard on the subject. We looked at the issue from all angles— were meetings too long, too short, or what? Some of us concluded that we had too many and most of them weren't very productive.

"At that point," says Tom, "it was tempting to say 'Well, we solved that one,' and walk out. But we didn't let anybody off the hook until someone volunteered to try and solve the issue by a certain time. Unfortunately," he added, "in that case, they volunteered me."

Solving problems. Senior Program Director Tom Lee leads one of many GEBIC storyboarding sessions, where team members visually brainstorm issues and problems and then generate creative solutions.

The teams learned later how to fine-tune their operations with a more sophisticated version of storyboarding, called process mapping. The specific exercise was a concept called "Customer Experience Mapping" developed by William J. Diffley of Diffley Associates, Madison, Connecticut.

Again on a wall board, every step in a process is recorded on a pyramid of cards, organized sequentially with strings pinned between them to show the interaction and flow of functions. You first map your concept, and then validate it from the point of view of customer experience.

The wall display gives the impression of cobwebs strung by a nearsighted spider. It is an allusion that might please Jack Welch. He has continually urged GE people to "get rid of thousands of bad habits accumulated since the creation of General Electric." Then, in a question that stirs up the dusty clouds of memory, he asks: "Would you like to move from a house after 112 years? Think of what would be in the closets and the attic."

One of the major benefits process mapping brings is to visually unfold, often for the first time, the best way to view and improve an operation from start to finish. It suggests how it can be measured by efficiency, resource allocation, productivity, or whatever.

Ironically, when GEBIC's manager—John Wilfore—was learning the techniques of process mapping to improve his management skills, he was in the midst of transferring much of his own management control to the people of GEBIC.

Gary Martini also opened the door for them to enter another world of problem solving: paradigms.

The term stems from the Greek word which means an example, a model, or a pattern. TIME magazine notes that business today uses paradigm "as a sort of reality thresher — a way of comparing past and present, an implement for sorting out history at a moment of tumbling global change."

Gary Martini told them, "this can be a potent instrument to control change at GEBIC. Your challenge will be to recognize your paradigms and not be limited by them."

You can visualize a paradigm, he said, as "a set of rules for success, things that have worked in the past . . . or boundaries which you've set for yourself. Because the old rules have worked in the past, you usually think that if you use them again, you'll eventually get to where you want to go.

"The problem with that," said Gary, "is that a rigid set of rules will very likely cause you to miss some new opportunities. Even worse, you'll tend to filter out new inputs because they don't fit your comfortable old paradigm."

As an example, he related the image that most Americans had of Japanese products in the '50s: junk, as portrayed in Joel Barker's video, "Discovering the Future . . . the Business of Paradigms." Today, of course, people have discarded the old paradigm and have replaced it with a new one: Japanese products mean expensive, high tech products.

"Now, if you consider your present paradigms at GEBIC," Martini told them, "you *are* living in a box. The walls are made up of all those old rules and standards you've followed over the years. Those boundaries and barriers have turned your box— your paradigms— into a trap, limiting your mind to new ideas.

"It's unusual when a whole company, like GE, tries to trade in old paradigms for new ones, and change its culture," said Martini. "An article in the *New York Times* indicated that IBM vowed to do that also in the fall of 1991, when for the first time they endorsed 'open systems,' which allow computers made by different firms to interact. Carl J. Conti, the firm's senior vice president at the time, in charge of developing big computers and their software said, 'I would characterize this announcement— along with other things we've done— as representative of a paradigm shift.'

"That," added Martini, "is the kind of fundamental change you'll have to make in your thinking if you want GEBIC to become a self-directed work force. Put behind you those days of waiting for someone to tell you what to do and how to do it.

"The new skills you're learning will help you set your own standards. You'll want that because you're the ones who are going to have to get GEBIC moving. The old days of 'somebody ought to' are gone. That somebody is now you."

Program Director Cherie Lussier is convinced the new skills have helped alter their old paradigms. "We come up with answers much more quickly now. We discuss things as a team, and then act on them. No one has to tell us 'Here's how it's done.' "

Another program director, Carol Van Riper, refers to what they've learned as 'life skills' because they're valuable in personal as well as professional relationships. "They help you adapt, and be more sensitive in dealing with children, parents, whomever."

John Wilfore shakes his head and smiles when he recalls the sessions on group dynamics and problem solving. "Gary told Richard and me up front that 'you can't make cultural change until people have the skills.' We were convinced after our sessions with him. Honestly, you could almost hear the noise of our teams as we revved up the engines of change."

The people of GEBIC found that it was much easier to swing into operation once they had sharpened their skills and increased their inventory of tools. They began by focusing on objectives, identifying tasks, and then moving out to get the job done.

The make-up of the GEBIC teams stemmed from the four, crisp mission statements formulated earlier. The mission of the first aligned both with this commitment and with Costello's initial charter to keep the customer foremost: "Each of us is dedicated to providing *easy access* to GE's commercial, industrial and technical products and services."

One of the first moves the Easy Access team made was to rationalize the needs of the customer. Those needs, not surprisingly, matched those of GEBIC's people when they themselves set out to buy something by phone. Their conclusion: easy access meant one phone number; someone who could help, and who cared; a timely response; and promises kept.

GEBIC's Easy Access team knew they had their work cut out for them, because customers perceive GE for what it really is— a big, complex company that's often hard to do business with. It's sobering to realize that one hundred million people call GE every year. Furthermore, a sizeable chunk of them have trouble reaching people who can help.

"It was a dual challenge," says Loretta Wilary. "We wanted to satisfy GE customers, but at the same time, we couldn't forget the needs of the 13 GE businesses we serve."

The Easy Access team, therefore, established two program objectives. The primary one aimed at customers— prove the company's commitment to them through added values provided by GEBIC. One extra value was proposed at GEBIC's visioning session: a toll-free number, and multilingual access for GE customers outside the U.S.

Their second objective was to make people *within* GE more aware of the GEBIC resources available to them. This would boost sales and marketing productivity and, in the process, enhance each component's ability to serve GE customers, whether its own or customers of sister components.

The wheels began to turn. GEBIC's vision of a globalized, toll-free information center for GE became a reality. The

---

Initial Team Objectives

Easy Access
> Purpose is to identify, develop and implement a communications plan resulting in increased GE accessibility and better awareness and understanding of GEBIC.

Sharing Knowledge/Continuous Training
> Purpose is to recognize and address initial and on-going training requirements of the Center, enabling us to perform our job functions more effectively by focusing our efforts on our mutual sharing of knowledge and best practices.

Accurate Answers/Technology
> Purpose is to develop and integrate appropriate tools and resources to facilitate the delivery of accurate answers to caller inquiries in a timely and efficient manner.

Rewards & Compensation
> Purpose is to recommend and establish a reward and compensation program that is based on established measurements, that reward GEBIC members for desired performance.

Springboard for action. Four statements in GEBIC's mission lead to the formation of focused teams which define their own separate objectives, and then set out to fulfill them.

former telephone tollgate, a commercial line, was switched in 1991 to an 800 number. Jacquie Braam, who speaks Spanish fluently, joined the staff when GEBIC created and installed another toll-free number to serve the emerging Mexican marketplace. Carol Van Riper provides back-up. GEBIC also subscribed to AT&T's Language Line,® gaining additional translation support for other languages.

The Easy Access team recognized that they should also prime GE people about the support available from GEBIC. So they made sure the word got to those GE people who contact customers—in marketing, sales, service and tele-marketing, receptionists and secretaries, switchboard operators, communicators, and so on.

By monitoring call volume, the team identified promising areas for special emphasis. This led to new programs for product training, call handling, business reviews, plant tours, management presentations, and information exchanges.

The focus of Easy Access then shifted to the outside world, targeting buyers, specifiers, engineers, middle management, consultants and exporters. As a result, GE customers and prospects could hardly go about their business without bumping into the word from GEBIC. Listings for the center appeared in magazines and buyers guides, in literature at trade shows and conferences, in phone books, buyers guides such as the Thomas Register, and the like.

The intent of the messages was the same: let customers know that GE people care about them, and that GEBIC can make it easier for them to do business with GE through "one stop" shopping.

The aims of the Sharing Knowledge team came from GEBIC's second mission statement: "We believe in sharing knowledge and the pursuit of continuous learning. Our bywords are adaptability, flexibility and team work."

The team targeted three tasks: standardize training methods for both present staff and new hires; sharpen call handling and operational procedures; and seek the help of GE businesses in satisfying customers who call GEBIC.

As one of their first moves, the team took to heart Gary Martini's tips on group dynamics. Members prepared and distributed an 11-page Meeting Handbook that reminded everyone, in no-nonsense fashion, how to keep their work on track.

"Meetings are not going to go away!" the handbook exhorted. But, "when meeting time is used wisely, no one seems to mind." It then pierced to the heart of the matter: "Remember when we never had meetings? How effective were the communications then?

"If we have productive meetings where agendas are clear, action plans put into place, and with resulting accomplishments, then we will have made progress," the handbook concluded. It then showed the reader, step by step, how to conduct a productive meeting.

This was no philosophical tract. Rather, it was a pragmatic diary produced by experienced practitioners.

Even with the help of the handbook, Gary Martini predicted that future teams at GEBIC would have a hard time keeping up with the current team. "On a scale of one to 10, the staff is at level seven in understanding the phenomena of what happens during a meeting, and why," he said.

The team recognized early on that they would have to upgrade their informal approach to training if they were

Key to training. New members, like John Madigan (left), find their transition into GEBIC is smoother and faster because of mentoring by veterans such as Program Director Marie Murray.

to bring new program directors quickly and smoothly into the GEBIC business cycle. So the Sharing Knowledge team initiated a mentoring program to prop up the learning curve of new hires. Each was paired with a veteran who provided counsel and advice as needed.

Over time, this was supplemented with orientation sessions, which ultimately extended over a full week. "We noticed the difference right away," says Loretta Wilary. "Our new people settled in with us faster and better than ever before."

In time, the newer hires suggested that they redesign the transition process. Based on their own experiences and success, they factored in individual needs of newcomers to provide constructive feedback, and other actions that made the newcomers feel "at home" sooner.

The new program directors dispelled one myth. The dictates of tradition had long held that extensive GE experience was mandatory to perform call handling.

"That was nonsense," says David Cairns, who came to GE in March 1991 with another recruit, Kevin Vaughn. "It's much more important to hire people who know how to deal with customers, using the latest in information technology. I knew that GE made light bulbs and appliances when I joined, and that was about all. But after eight weeks of training, I'll bet Kevin and I knew more about the scope of the company than the average long-term employee."

"I'm sure David is right," confirms GEBIC's specialist for office administration, Evie DiDonato, who came to GEBIC shortly after it was formed in 1984. "Some program directors did have GE experience and it helped. But even those off the street became what I'd call GE experts in no time at all."

One of the major GEBIC advances in productivity came in early 1990, in the form of notes on the back of a beverage napkin. Over lunch with Richard Costello, members of the Sharing Knowledge team wondered if a computer program could be prepared that would in a matter of minutes bring on screen the options a program director could apply to a caller's question. They all felt the promise was worth pursuing.

Outside consultants said it would take months and a big budget to develop the program. But in one week, GEBIC team members conceptualized and developed an on-line, real-time system called Playbook which uses existing software and hardware.

According to Tom Lee, "it's really a crude form of artificial intelligence to access information, which we modify on a continuous basis. Our present Playbook is third generation. We use it daily to address call handling and the answers to complex issues, plus operational procedures, coding, team-building and the like."

Accurate Answers formed the focus of the third team, again stemming from GEBIC's mission: "We, as a team of GE professionals, provide personalized attention and accurate answers." In effect, their goal was to have the answer ready before the customer asked the question.

As one of its first tasks, the team analyzed calls to see how best to handle them. Incoming questions covered the spectrum of information: Where to buy. Price and delivery. Product application and after-sale support. Literature or specifying data. Repair or replacement service. And, that old bugaboo that gives so many companies a bad name — the identification and ordering of spare or renewal parts,

```
<SEQ>    0000
<SUBJ>

                    **** GEBIC ****
                    ** PLAYBOOK **

Visualize the Training Manual that will result from our collective
efforts as a "GEBIC PLAYBOOK"; the process that enables us to do
our jobs effectively through common understanding of GEBIC
definitions and procedures.

The caller initiates the "play", we use our knowledge, and common
definition of the "PLAYBOOK" to respond to and answer the caller.
With our knowledge we complete the "Play", as defined by the "PLAYBOOK",
improvising and/or adapting as required.

To access the entire PLAYBOOK on GEFILE:

   At the $ prompt, type "PB" and press the return key twice. This will

                                              Document 1 of 4
BROWSE> █
```

Rich desserts. "Playbook," conceived during a GEBIC luncheon meeting with Richard Costello, is an on-line electronic resource that helps program directors speed answers to complex questions posed by callers.

even for discontinued products and lines GE has sold to other companies.

Before the self-direction process began, management decided to create a new layer of people to reinforce the call handling of program directors. Three newcomers— Julie Dinardo, Karen Malaczynski and Marie Murray— were brought in as customer service representatives, exclusively to "screen" calls for the more experienced program directors.

Their job was to handle by themselves the easy incoming calls— the "defaults"— and refer any which required more extensive research to the program directors. If the latter were busy, the "screeners" left a written memo for follow-up.

Theoretically, the system made sense in the interests of efficiency. But it made no sense to GEBIC operations nor to the customers whose inquiries smoldered at the bottom of the stacks of handwritten memos which piled up during the heat of battle on program directors' desks.

The concept made no sense either to the "screeners." They knew that with some additional training, they could easily grow to become full-fledged program directors. And it certainly made no sense in the most obvious result— the two-tiered phone system further fanned the flames of the "we vs. they" climate that had been so prevalent. After a few months into the team-building process with its lively, open discussions, the screening process was scrapped.

A major goal of the Accurate Answers team was to provide resources for call handling, which covered a wide spectrum: data on products, services and GE businesses; information about contacts; product catalogs for existing and discontinued products and services, etc. The team also developed procedures for equipping all program directors with the same resources, as well as methods for soliciting and updating inputs from the GE businesses.

An analysis by the Accurate Answers team found that with two-thirds of the inquiries, program directors could complete the call loops on their own. With a keystroke, they could access mainframe databases through software customized to GEBIC needs.

However, one out of every three inquiries called for further GE back-up. There is plenty available now, but it wasn't always that way.

When GEBIC opened its GE front door to callers in 1984, it fielded inquiries with four people and a paper database. Over the years, it established ties with GE people who could help tackle the more difficult issues. Today, GEBIC is linked to a network of almost 3,000 contact points including specialists in products, sales and service. GEBIC's database, which is constantly being updated, provides access to 120 GE components, 1800 sales and service operations, and 2,000 distributors.

The fourth GEBIC team, Rewards and Compensation, responded to the portion of the mission which stated, "We foster a dynamic and rewarding environment, built upon mutual respect and support."

In simplest terms, according to team member Jacquie Braam, "it said that our job was to take the temperature of Team GEBIC. We wanted to know what our own needs were, provide for them, and devise a fair way to reward improved performance."

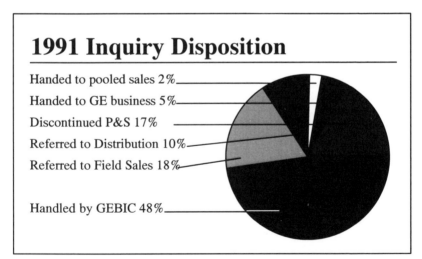

1991 Inquiry Disposition

Handed to pooled sales 2%

Handed to GE business 5%

Discontinued P&S 17%

Referred to Distribution 10%

Referred to Field Sales 18%

Handled by GEBIC 48%

Handling inquiries. Almost two thirds of incoming calls, including those about discontinued GE offerings, are handled by GEBIC program directors. One of every three calls, however, requires expert help that is supplied by other contacts within the company upon referral by GEBIC.

Most GEBIC measurements were relics from the earlier days of GEBIC. So the Rewards and Compensation team searched for more contemporary yardsticks.

Shortly after the Orlando session in the fall of 1989, Wilfore worked with the team to devise a crude peer evaluation form as an interim tool. Everyone rated each other, and the results were reviewed first with the individuals, then shared in summary form with the group.

Giving and receiving feedback, both positive and constructive, is difficult in itself. And while the data is enlightening, it doesn't always leave the recipients feeling good.

So the Rewards and Compensation team met with Wilfore to suggest that maybe the members of GEBIC should evaluate his performance. It seemed like a good way to lay before him constructive suggestions on his behavior, as he had done concerning theirs.

Once again, Martini was asked to help. This time, he brought to bear his copyrighted "Calibration-Team Building" model.

The GEBIC employees knew, of course, that as with any human being, their manager had his strengths and limitations. But as Martini helped them dig to the roots of existing concerns and problems, they discovered that the cause of much of their uneasiness and discontent came from their own limitations amd interactions. They were also genuinely surprised to discover how positive everyone felt about each other, including their individual contributions.

The meeting plumbed to the heart of the meaning suggested by "calibration": finding a balance between positive feedback and constructive criticism. It also marked more progress toward the open and honest environment the team had been striving for. Wilfore reinforced the outcome with another move, which was as symbolic as it was practical: he had a new doorway cut between his office and the back offices of the other team members. It worked both ways: the team had access to him and he had access to the team.

The contrast between the new GEBIC and the GEBIC before self-direction was not lost on team members. In the hierarchical era, employees who wanted to talk to the center manager first had to make an appointment, then circle through the front lobby to reach the manager's office.

Such meetings were rare. Even though the organization was quite small, meetings with upper management, or with peers, were even more rare. A cross-functional dialogue between the two major functions— program directors and support staff— was non-existent.

Even GEBIC's main purpose, serving customers and GE businesses, was subverted by the boundaries of the hierarchy. With the exception of an occasional trade show, employees were rarely allowed to deal with outsiders as representatives of the center.

The calibration session between Wilfore and the others in GEBIC proved a health-giving catharsis. It blew away some choking clouds of distrust and misunderstanding. It also underscored as in their session at Orlando that they needed the contributions of all team members, including those of John Wilfore, if they were to successfully transform their business.

In another aspect of the calibration session, the various teams met to recount their progress to date, and collectively to begin identifying obstacles and preparing action plans to overcome them. The Rewards and Compensation team hoped that new measurements would be a by-product.

A recurring question at the meeting with Martini was: "As a team, how are we doing?" The GEBIC people expressed great pride in their progress over a year and a half and, above all, hoped that Gary would tell them they were "there."

But Gary Martini reminded them, as he had before, that their journey was just that— a journey. The benefits, he said, would come more from the journey than from the destination.

One member of GEBIC summed up the frustration of them all: "But how are we supposed to know how much we've grown or changed?" So Gary related a personal experience that helped put things in perspective.

"My father-in-law used to come and visit me about every six months. On one visit, he brought a small blue spruce tree. I nurtured and watered it and did everything the books say to do. But I could never see it grow or notice that anything had changed.

"Every time my father-in-law visited, he would tell me, 'My, that blue spruce has really grown.' But I always said that it looked to me as if it hadn't grown at all. Then he'd respond, 'You're too close to it to notice any change.'

"And that," said Gary, "is symbolic of the growth and change that's happening right here at GEBIC. You grow each day but you're too close to see it; I come every three or four months and I see significant growth. It's just like the blue spruce.

"The progress you've made," he added, "is good for both of us. I've actually learned as much here because of it as I did getting my Master's degree at Case Western in Cleveland."

Shortly thereafter, Gary Martini returned to GEBIC with a living reminder of the changes which were occurring— a

A living metaphor. "It's hard for you to see the progress you've made," says Gary Martini. "This blue spruce tree will serve as a daily reminder of the continuing growth you're making."

blue spruce tree to serve as a living metaphor for the
GEBIC team. "Your team is much like this blue spruce
tree," he said, in a planting ceremony in front of the office
building. "From day to day, the rate of growth is quite
small. Yet from month to month, both grow quite tall."

The Rewards and Compensation team still struggled to
find a practical way to recognize, reward and compensate
GEBIC people for their accelerating progress. Separately,
Richard Costello, John Wilfore and team member Susan
Moyer initiated a search on their own.

Strangely, the latter group met quietly behind closed doors.

It suggested there was at least one more detour ahead
before the road to self-direction would straighten and
become well defined.

Step Four:
Taking Stock

Action, GEBIC hoped, would beget progress. But it wasn't so sure.

To find out how much progress had been made, the Rewards and Compensation team felt it should devise additional forms of measurement. And, to keep the flywheel of action spinning, it planned to squirt on a dab of recognition and reward now and then.

In the past, the accepted form of measurement for GEBIC had been tonnage—in the telemarketing business, that meant call volume. Due to the efforts of the Easy Access

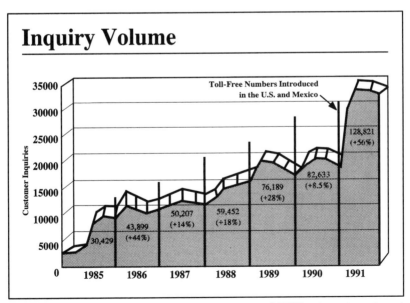

Inquiry Volume

Toll-Free Numbers Introduced in the U.S. and Mexico

30,429	
43,899 (+44%)	
50,207 (+14%)	
59,452 (+18%)	
76,189 (+28%)	
82,633 (+8.5%)	
128,821 (+56%)	

Call volume: up and up. The steady rise in calls to GEBIC gets a sharp boost when two "visioning" goals are achieved—toll-free service and the beginning of GEBIC globalization with extension into Mexico.

team, call volume began to rise. Close behind, ascending in lockstep, came the need for more program directors.

The Rewards and Compensation team members decided they should spruce up the old measurements by tailoring something new. They began by searching for the factor that was most important to the success of their business.

It didn't take much intuition or probing to discern that the average customer who called GEBIC had not the remotest interest in call volume. Instead, customers were interested in the same goals other GEBIC teams were already converging on— easy access and accurate answers.

Members of GEBIC didn't need a blue spruce tree, either, to see that their business should aim at the very target Richard Costello had identified at the beginning of their journey: the satisfied customer. They hoped to share the conviction of the happy owner of a Dell computer who told *The New York Times*, "If you talk directly to the

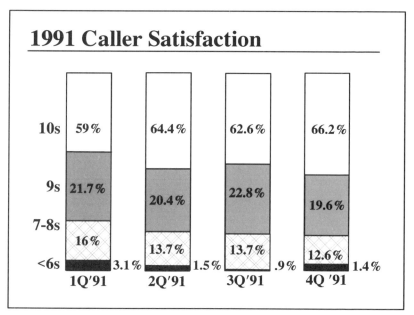

1991 Caller Satisfaction

	1Q'91	2Q'91	3Q'91	4Q '91
10s	59%	64.4%	62.6%	66.2%
9s	21.7%	20.4%	22.8%	19.6%
7-8s	16%	13.7%	13.7%	12.6%
<6s	3.1%	1.5%	.9%	1.4%

Callers like GEBIC service, according to call-back surveys. Two of every three give GEBIC a perfect score on a scale of one to 10, while one of every five gives a score of nine. Only one in a hundred now reports any problem or dissatisfaction.

customer you can genuinely add value ... people will buy your stuff and give you a margin that you can live with."

During a telephone interview conducted by an outside market research firm, nearly two out of every three callers gave GEBIC a perfect score on a scale of one to 10. One of every five proffered a score of nine. Only one of every

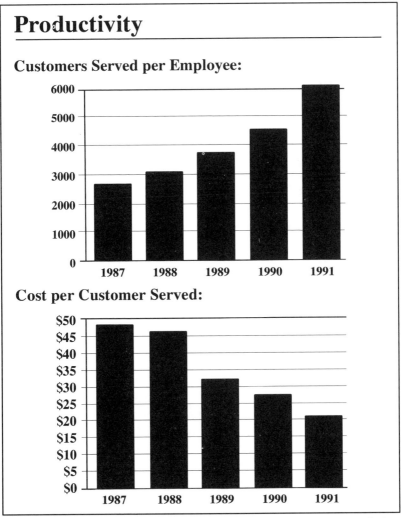

Productivity

Customers Served per Employee:

Cost per Customer Served:

The crucial issue. The number of customers served per employee climbs, while the cost per customer declines. This propels cost-based productivity up 106% over the three-year period from 1989 to 1991.

hundred callers said they were not completely satisfied with the response they received.

Callers also were asked to rate GEBIC program directors on attitudes, communication skills, thoroughness and understanding. Numeric scores were complemented with the verbatim comments of customers.

Originally, program directors saw only their own evaluations. But they soon recognized that each could benefit by reviewing all the others. They soon shared scores and lessons learned that helped upgrade everyone's performance.

While it was nice to look good on the outside, GEBIC felt it probably ought to take its own temperature, too. Happily, it found that its operational health was improving. Call volume was still rising, but employees were intrigued to find that the need for more program directors was going up at a slower pace.

This meant that productivity — their measure of success that was second only in importance to quality, or customer satisfaction — had to be going up. And it was.

Customers served per employee had gone up 53% in just two years — from 3,698 in 1989 to 6,105 in 1991. During that same period, the cost per customer served had plummeted by 34% — from $31.76 to $20.80.

Clearly, the self-directed work team concept was taking hold at GEBIC.

An accelerating business normally kicks up problems. GEBIC was no exception.

In late 1989, Susan Moyer, GEBIC's program manager — communications, projected that calls to GEBIC in 1990 from listings in Thomas Register alone would double over the previous year — an additional 250 calls per week. She predicted that total calls to GEBIC would go up 50 percent during that same period.

At that time, there wasn't much room for expansion. Marie Murray recalls talking to "21,000 customers over a period of two years. That's an average of 45 to 50 calls a day. The number later jumped as high as 70 calls a day after we put in the toll-free number."

Team members became concerned that this pressure on GEBIC people might fester into a motivational problem. So they solicited common-sense fixes.

Tom Lee proposed scheduling non-telephone tasks during slower call periods. Marie Murray pointed out the obvious: consolidate call-handling aids closer to the point of use. And Chris Berglund noted that members were more likely to participate in team-related or mentoring projects in early mornings rather than in busier afternoons.

But the more basic issue remained: improved measurement of GEBIC performance, coupled with suitable recognition and reward.

The intent of the sessions which Richard Costello, John Wilfore and Sue Moyer had been holding behind closed doors was to determine how the previous, annual, caller satisfaction surveys by an outside market research firm could be updated and made more relevant to the new team environment.

As a result of the deliberations, several significant changes were made. The annual telephone surveys, which once a year disclosed how GEBIC was performing, expanded to an on-going program— 100 interviews per program director per quarter, conducted within two days after callers contacted GEBIC.

They also modified the reporting of the one to 10 rating structure, stressing the goal of perfect scores of 10 as the measure of customer satisfaction, rather than reporting "averages."

Behind-the-scenes meetings between Richard Costello and John Wilfore had begun shaping their version of a bonus program to serve as the fulcrum in the measurement process. They made all of the classic management moves— they holed up behind closed doors to sort out the issues and alternatives, called in consultants, devised a system that would measure everybody sixteen ways from Sunday, and so on.

During the second quarter of the year, they emerged to unveil their program to the people of GEBIC. They were welcomed about as warmly as two competitors who, by accident, had wandered into a GE family reunion.

"Along with all of the classic moves," recalls Costello, "John and I made all of the classic mistakes. The problem at base was that we didn't know if the system we had proposed was right or not, probably because we didn't answer the phones nor understand the full impact on people.

"Anyway, we started out with the best of intentions. But we had initiated a kind of power game in the mold of the old-fashioned manager. You know how that goes: 'This is important stuff, so we're not going to involve the employees.'

"We thought about tying incentives to salaries," said Costello. "Then, to top it off, we planned to give incentives to some GEBIC people, but not all—a kind of pay-for-performance program. Implicit in the concept was a battle among peers, promoting individualism and even superstars. The net effect was that everyone would be in it for themselves."

If there's one characteristic of a self-directed work force, says John Wilfore, it is that members are not bashful. "They told us in no uncertain terms that if we gave reports and incentives to phone people only and not the others, it would widen the 'We vs. They' gap we'd all been trying so hard to close.

"Their clincher was that our key measurement, customer satisfaction, is achieved because of what everybody does, not what's done by just one individual or one group. That's true, of course. So the only conclusion one could draw was that there should be but one measurement for GEBIC and the incentive had to be team pay, not pay for the individual."

To underscore this point, the other members made sure that Wilfore, as a participating member of the team, would share equally with them in performance awards.

Mike Marchi, who was among the support people at the time, remembers that the program directors—who would have gained special status in the Costello/Wilfore program—stood up strongly for their compatriots in the support group. "At first, some leaned toward the proposal made by Richard and John. But at the end, they stood behind us 100% because of the support they knew we brought to their work and, as a result, to improving customer satisfaction."

Costello and Wilfore closed ranks with the Rewards and Compensation team in deciding on their next move: hire an outside consulting firm to create an appropriate bonus program for GEBIC.

In short order, GEBIC received development proposals from two reputable, well-established firms covering a time span of from six to 18 months and a cost of from $50,000 to $75,000. "Outrageous!" was the verdict of the team members. "Why not let *us* develop the program, and we'll use the money we save to fund the incentive bonuses?"

Good question. A central concept of the self-directed work force is to tell everybody everything. Why not take this action and the team members would know everything because they'd be the ones developing the bonus program?

Gary Martini concurred in the decision that the team should take the lead role. "Looking back, it obviously was the right way to go. The proposals had been made by two of the finest and most respected compensation consulting firms in the U.S. Yet the GEBIC Rewards and Compensation team settled down and developed a fine bonus program on their own. They called me a couple of times for advice, but that was the end of it. My role was minimal."

The Rewards & Compensation team put in place three guidelines for their deliberations. First, teamwork would override individual effort. Second, the bonus program would focus on meaningful business issues. And third, rewards would be linked to customer measurement.

Teamwork, the members had discovered, was the major distinction between an old-line, hierarchical GE organization and a high-involvement, self-directed work force. Hierarchy divided responsibility by *individual*; the self-directed work force placed responsibility squarely on the shoulders of the *team*.

Evie DiDonato observes that "each of us used to stay within the strict guidelines laid down by our manager. We were really individuals working in the same place instead of individuals working as a team. Some people liked that, and didn't want to change. They, and others who wanted only to work as individual contributors, couldn't survive in this teamwork mode, and left."

Of course, not all aspects of self-directed teamwork contribute to easy measurement. As Margi Call notes, "Sometimes the confusion of the team takes away from what we could accomplish as individuals. That's particularly true since we usually— although not always— try to reach a consensus in what we want to do.

"Teamwork actually slows down individual plans at times. But we gain more than we give away. Other people's thoughts expand our own base of ideas, along with our perception of solutions to the challenges we grapple with as a team."

The second guideline— identifying key business issues— prompted the Rewards & Compensation team to borrow a technique from their earlier "visioning" session. All GEBIC people split into four sub-teams, which met independently to identify issues and develop plans. The groups then reassembled to present their findings. Finally, the Rewards and Compensation team incorporated the best features of each into a single plan, with common goals for GEBIC.

They chose the same base point from which team GEBIC had launched all of its ventures: customer satisfaction. From a business point of view, they concluded that compensation should be controlled by two parameters— quality and call volume.

Quality was a given. For them, as for all members of GE, CEO Jack Welch had identified quality as a primary focus for the company in the '90s. Of more immediate importance, quality— i.e., customer satisfaction— was the reason GEBIC had been established.

The other parameter— call volume— in reality was tied to cost per call, as Costello had noted early on. That yielded a measurement of productivity.

By putting on track the first two guidelines— teamwork, and a focus on business issues— the group knew they would then have the needed mechanism to carry out the third guideline— linking rewards to measurement.

For the initial phase planned for the last half of 1990, the team elected to provide variable incentives to achieve the desired levels of quality and call volume. They had already hammered into place the target for quality: achieve or maintain perfect scores— 10s on their scale of one to 10— and reduce scores in the one to six range. These became the first two parts of a three-part program.

The initial band width matrix formulated by the team was a model of clarity and simplicity. It pegged desired quality at a higher level than that achieved by other major business-to-business information centers operated by such companies as AT&T, Dupont and IBM. It recognized reality— disruptive blips that would show up on GEBIC's operational radar, such as new phone people beginning their transition into the system, the introduction of the new toll-free GEBIC number, and the extension of service to Mexico.

The last program element targeted for the second stage of the program in 1991 was volume: maintain or improve quality levels of caller satisfaction while increasing volume loads. The latter would measure healthy gains in productivity.

The team made it clear the two parameters did *not* give GEBIC a one-or-the-other choice. "We must do both!" they exhorted. The only exception would be when call volume was increasing dramatically. Then GEBIC could either increase the quality level while maintaining the current call volume, or maintain quality while increasing call volume.

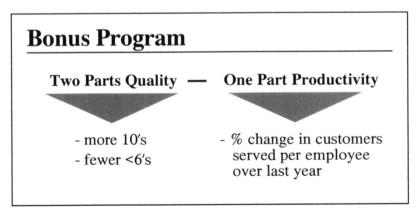

Bonus Program

Two Parts Quality — One Part Productivity

- more 10's
- fewer <6's

- % change in customers served per employee over last year

Base point for a bonus. GEBIC's Rewards and Compensation team members devise a program controlled by two important business parameters: quality, relating to customer satisfaction; and productivity, relating to customers served and cost per call.

For ease and clarity of measurement, the team developed a bonus matrix with specific thresholds and per cent payouts. They looked at previous data, analyzed achievements in the light of capacity deficits, calculated possible payouts for past periods, and documented their recommendations and goals for review and approval by management.

The outline of the GEBIC bonus program was lean and aggressive, yet elegant. It anticipated a maximum eight per cent bonus payout, which translated into 2.6% of GEBIC's total operating budget.

The aim of the bonus program fashioned by GEBIC's Rewards and Compensation team was right on target.

Each member of the GEBIC team, including John Wilfore, shared in a quarterly payout representing three per cent of their annual salary. The total cost to the center for the first year was still less than the outside development cost would have been if the GEBIC team had not taken on the responsibility to "do it ourselves."

The payoff, however, came in forms other than mere money.

"Of course, money talks," says David Cairns. "But the program serves as a watchdog that ensures no one will coast while the others do all the work. Even more important, it focuses us on what's important and motivates us to do a better job.

"We don't just do *things*; we get feedback from customers that tells us how well we're doing and whether or not we're improving. I think that's great."

There's an old saying in GE that "What you reward is what you get." The distribution of the first bonus checks in October 1990, reflecting the strong performance of GEBIC, indicated that GE was getting its money's worth.

VI

Step Five:
Unleashing the Power of Empowerment
■

Team GEBIC roared off under its own power sometime during the latter part of 1990, according to John Wilfore. "I'm not sure of the exact date and I can't pinpoint any one thing that triggered the ignition. But there's no question that the team got under way with the throttle wide open."

Wilfore believes the catalyst, if he were forced to choose one, would have to be GEBIC's mission, fashioned during an earlier stage of the process. "Everything we've done since then has focused on what's important, as documented in that statement.

"The mission identified four major objectives, which suggested priority areas of work. We then formed four teams, assumed responsibility to address those needs, and set about doing the tasks.

"In effect," said John, with a lingering trace of disbelief, "the teams took over the operational aspects of the Center."

Julie Dinardo confirms that the mission statement served as a roadmap for their journey. "It was essential to everything we did," she says.

It's interesting to note that while the composition and tasks of the teams have changed, the mission statement has remained immutable. So has the tagline that concludes the statement: "Committed to excellence, our customers and each other." The sentence gains credibility over time, along with a cryptic footnote which John Wilfore jotted at the bottom: "GEBIC's definition of Work-Out."

The mission statement also serves as the fulcrum for one-on-one goal planning, devised by the Rewards and Compensation team. Instead of the old performance appraisal system, where direction and steps were spelled out by the manager, GEBIC people now set their own goals and course. Every quarter, they set and review their own goals and progress with Wilfore, bask in the glow of knowing they've done something important and have done it well, then tweak their objectives to a higher trajectory for the next quarter.

In most regards, this one-on-one goal planning replaces the annual performance reviews that were for so long a part of the GE tradition. Of course, as manager, Wilfore still has to ship upstairs the hallowed personnel documents required by GE Human Resources. Susan Moyer, who has journeyed through both eras, dryly observes: "That's corporate stuff. GE needs *some* glue."

Clearly, some factor was acting as a prime mover on GEBIC. That force was empowerment. GEBIC's people often call it by another name: freedom.

"In my past job," says Cherie Lussier, "I often wondered why people who do the work couldn't be part of the decision-making process." Chris Berglund emphasizes that they are a part of it now at GEBIC. "There's no one looking over your shoulder. Of course, we have to live or die by what decisions we make. But if we want to do something, we talk about it and then just go do it."

Freedom breeds high involvement, Program Director Steve McKinlay is convinced. "Our newest people are just getting their feet on the ground and don't know what's going on yet. But they sense that it's really different at GEBIC and are excited about finding out how much control they can have."

Valerie McCormick, a program director who joined GEBIC late in 1991, sees only one problem with her new-found freedom at GEBIC: "There's so much I want to do, I don't have time for it all."

Most people at GEBIC exude the same spirit. Deb Reutter, who's on temporary duty, gives one good reason why: "Do you know what they did for me when the team had a writing seminar? They got a temp for a temp— they brought someone in so I could join in instead of just being an outsider whose only contribution would be answering the phone. I couldn't believe it.

"At the last place I worked," she continues, "they were leery about letting me in on programs because I was just a secretary. But here," she says, "when I ask Loretta or Steve or Roz and the others if they want to look over my work, they just say: 'Deb, we trust you.' It's a shock, but it tells me I can grow and learn and feel more secure."

Linda McClain credits her two years at GEBIC for "letting me spread my wings." She found it hard at first to adapt to the wide-open style of GEBIC meetings. "But after Loretta Wilary and I took facilitator training," she says, "we volunteered and were selected to conduct Work-Out sessions at a meeting of health-care managers from throughout GE, from Plastics to NBC. I would never have had the nerve to do that before, much less be invited."

GEBIC had begun to symbolize, with a better understanding of the process every day, what the editorial director of the *Harvard Business Review*, Alan Webber, calls "the egoless corporation." GEBIC people were acting in the manner ascribed by *Fortune* magazine to America's 100 fastest rising companies— responding "to customer wants and needs rather than letting managers arrogantly insist they instinctively know what's right."

Empowerment thrust on the people of GEBIC what GE CEO Jack Welch calls "that sense of ownership, that commitment to relentless personal interaction and immediate sharing of information." They were edging closer and closer to his goal of instilling "speed, simplicity and self-confidence in every person in the organization."

John Wilfore liked Welch's equation because while it was simple, it was potent. But for GEBIC he felt the order might be a bit different.

"With us, simplicity came first. That was mandated by delayering— it removed a whole layer of GEBIC managers. That brought about speed, because it opened up our lines of communication and interaction, and things started to heat up. Then, the more our people seized the reins of power that were made available to them, and the more they found that their solutions were as good if not better than anybody else's, the more they gained self-confidence."

As an afterthought, Wilfore says, "GEBIC reminds me of a breeder reactor. All the time it's on line it generates energy. And that energy continually refuels the reactor." Then he adds, with serious intent, "You know the theory of the breeder. It's supposed to produce more energy than it can use. I honestly believe that's happening at GEBIC, and my role now is to help channel it."

Simplicity is now the watchword in everything GEBIC does.

"Take our Caller Satisfaction Index, for example," says Susan Moyer. "We used to tabulate results every quarter. It required a mountain of paperwork, along with the handling that goes with it. But for continuous improvement, the phone people did not want to wait three months to see how they were doing. They asked, 'Why can't we see it sooner?' So the team began to work with the vendor and now it's automatic. With a new computer program, the program directors just push the button and the latest caller satisfaction ratings pop up on the screen."

```
MP8020PU   SM  I              CALLER SATISFACTION SURVEY                    05/06/92
2SR  -  69  -   528                 INQUIRY/MAINTENANCE                        10:56
CALL DATE 03/09/92  TIME 16:07  COMP GY7                        '     HSR REF 2463
                                      INSTALLATION & SERVICE ENGINEERING
GEBIC RATING  10
STEVE GAVE ME THE NUMBER I NEEDED QUICKLY. HE WAS HELPFUL. P NE


GE RATING     10
THE SERVICE WAS GREAT. THE REPAIR MAN CAME OUT AND FIXED EVERYTHING AND HE EVEN
STOPPED IN THE NEXT MORNING ON HIS OWN TIME TO MAKE SURE EVERYTHING WAS STILL
WORKING FINE. I AM VERY PLEASED WITH THE SERVICE I RECEIVED. P NE

CALLBACK IND  0  NONE


PD FOLLOW-UP:


MODIFY DATA AS DESIRED
```

Moving mountains. At the touch of a button, the current Caller Satisfaction Index replaces the "mountain of paperwork" formerly required to pull up this key data.

John Wilfore says this matches perfectly with the intent of GE's Work-Out. "Cutting out useless steps is just half the battle. We're supposed to *improve* the process, too."

Adds Susan Moyer, "at the same time, we shaped up our monthly reports. In some cases, we decided to send out word that we were cutting them out. Then, we sat back to see if anybody screamed. No one did, so now we just send a concise quarterly report, and that fills the bill just fine."

Evie DiDonato cites first-hand proof that GEBIC's self-directed work team has arrived at that state of simplicity, the "boundaryless business," which Jack Welch envisions. And, she says, "It's not only good for GE, but for me, too.

"I used to be pigeon-holed as a secretary. We each had a job description, and mine said I was to type and answer the phone." No more, she says. "Now I'm as much a member of the team as anybody else, and get involved in all kinds of projects to improve the way we serve customers and run our business.

"I don't have to ask John Wilfore about many things, because he's eliminated so much of the bureaucracy. Invoices, for example—I can approve up to $500. We've cut out a good many other useless steps, such as regular time records. We only report them when someone's out for an extended illness."

The only problem, according to Evie, is "there aren't enough hours in the day to do everything I want to get done. And I don't mind if days aren't always eight to five, because I'm treated like a professional, and face the same challenges that everyone else does. I'm on my own, but I'm always working with the others.

"It's great to have the boundaries come down," she concludes.

The people of GEBIC also concluded they ought to bring down the walls literally as well as figuratively. A large conference room which had physically divided people into separate office areas was removed, fulfilling their desire to work more closely together.

Rosalind Wilkins says she's also glad that she escaped the "trap" of her previous job, which involved doing work for a large number of people. "I posted several times to move up to a more responsible job, but was told nothing but secretarial work was available, which I don't think was the case.

"Then self-direction got under way. There was talk about getting temps to handle extra work. I said we didn't need to, that I could do it. John asked for a vote, and everybody raised their hands. So I got the job."

Mike Marchi notes that "GE managers talk about loosening up their control, but not many have empowered people to the extent that John Wilfore does." One technique, he notes, is to structure a business so tightly that there's no need for a manager. "That's not empowerment."

Another dodge is to authorize financial transactions up to a certain limit, but venture no farther into self-direction. "I know one manager," says Mike, "who tells his people, 'You can do anything you want, but check with me first.' That neither contributes to simplicity nor to self-confidence and self-direction."

Speed was another natural by-product of empowerment. The reason, according to Susan Moyer, was two-fold: "Before the self-direction process, we neither had the knowledge to know what was going on, nor the authority to get things done. Obviously, you can't be pro-active if you're uninformed and powerless. As individuals, we used to be isolated. But not any more."

Paul Chmielewski relates a recent problem with cellular phones. "In the old days, we'd take a problem to the manager who'd say, 'Fix it, and then come see me.' Now, we take care of it ourselves or refer it to one of our teams and before you know it, it's done."

GEBIC members brought to bear two tools to get things done in less time. The first, in the words of a recent report by the team, was "a comprehensive and business-relevant training program."

The people of GEBIC decided early on that there wasn't any point in waiting 20 years to hire program directors with long company experience. The selection criterion, they concluded, should instead be communication skills.

More and more, therefore, they hired new people from the outside.

They proposed another sharp change: why not let team members interview the candidates since they could equate more closely with the applicants and find out quickly how good they might be? It made sense, of course.

They also identified the qualities they knew were most important, such as team orientation, analytical problem solving, team achievements and computer simulation, and used competency-based interview guides secured from another GE team-focused component.

GEBIC people who conducted the interviews operated under a simple, new rule: "We only hire those who get our unanimous vote. We're not interested in average individuals, or average scores. The only real question is: 'Would we hire that individual?' "

If compatibility is the measure, it works. One new hire told Rosalind Wilkins, "I couldn't believe how quickly all of you made me feel at home. No wonder you're so happy here."

The second tool GEBIC wielded to make jobs easier was advanced technology. This choice was easy, because GEBIC people were being squeezed on one side by escalating call volume, and on the other by an increasing diversity of GE product lines.

GEBIC people melded their own creative efforts with those of outside information experts. As a result, GEBIC combined the output of three existing computer terminals that brought information resources to program directors into a single-screen, user-friendly system. This multifunctional capability again stems directly from GEBIC's mission: easy access— another way of saying speed— and accurate answers.

"There was some concern going in that speeding up things just meant more work," says Mike Marchi. "Actually, it made the job easier. It's hard to convince outsiders, but it's true.

"Once people realize there are fewer managers around, and that it's perfectly all right to move on their own, they figure out better ways to do things— they throw out unnecessary steps, consolidate, standardize, whatever."

Says Mike, "call the process by any name you want—empowerment, team-building, self-direction, Work-Out. It does speed things up. But people shouldn't be afraid of it. It's actually a great opportunity for them to upgrade their jobs, gain new skills, and make themselves more promotable and marketable."

Speed and simplicity generated a surge of self-confidence in GEBIC people in everything they did. It fueled the assurance that, to a large degree, they controlled their own destiny. They received high marks for this self-confidence by passing a crucial test in March 1991.

Since Richard Costello's operations were a part of GE's corporate staff, he reasoned that GEBIC should report on its role in the grand GE scheme of things to his boss, Frank P. Doyle. Doyle is GE's Senior Vice President for External and Industrial Relations and reports to CEO Jack Welch. Doyle suggested that Costello arrange for the presentation at his next extended staff meeting, when all of his managers would be in attendance.

Now, self-direction may be on the rise at GE, but traces of the old GE hierarchy remain. And one of those traces

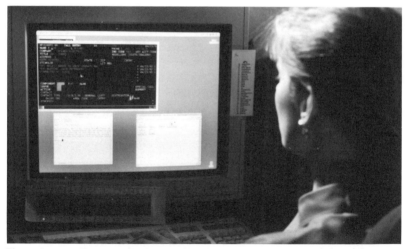

Three-in-one. The output of three existing computer terminals at GEBIC has been combined into a more user-friendly, single-screen system which makes call handling easier, faster and better.

shows up in the form of skittishness on the part of lower management when they're tabbed to report to upper management. The higher the level of management, the higher the level of skittishness.

What often happens is that the lower echelon defers to someone up the ladder to make the pitch, and the latter welcomes the opportunity because of the exposure to the executive office.

But Richard Costello and John Wilfore, in the true spirit of empowerment, decided to go back and ask the members of team GEBIC if, first, they would like to make the presentation and, second, whom among themselves they wanted to deliver GEBIC's message to Fairfield. The members accepted because they felt it would be a great oppor-

---

AGENDA:
Presentation to Senior GE Management

John Wilfore -- Introduction
- 30 years with GE
  - startup task force for GEBIC
- joined GEBIC in April 1986

Julie Dinardo -- Getting Started, The Evolution
- new GE employee, September 1989

Nora Richter -- The Process
- 10 years with GE
- TM startups at GEAC & Plastics SSC
- at GEBIC since February 1987

Steve McKinlay -- Moving From One Team To Another
- from GE's Lighting NCSC
- joined GEBIC in July 1990

Tom Lee -- Accomplishments & Results
- 14 years with GE
- purchasing with Power Generation business
- with GEBIC since March 1984

Going topside. For a GE executive office presentation, GEBIC team members prepare the agenda and content, and even decide who will deliver the messages to senior management and staff.

tunity to let GE management know that the word was getting through. "There isn't one wallflower in the whole group," says Wilfore. "Their self-confidence was and is amazing."

As GEBIC manager, John was expected to be there, along with Richard Costello, to make the introductions. But the people of GEBIC decided on the make-up of the presentation team—four of their members, plus John. Two of them were veterans, with 10 and 14 years of service with GE. The others were newcomers to GEBIC—one had been there a year and a half, the other less than a year.

At the meeting, they told Doyle and his assemblage, "we're here to report that change and empowerment work." Then they described "what it takes and how it feels to make change happen" on the way to becoming a self-directed work force.

Julie Dinardo, who had been with GE for only slightly more than a year, related the rocky start of their early evolution—"learning about ourselves and each other, discovering that differences were not only O.K. but desirable."

Nora Richter, who spent six years in telemarketing start-up operations at GE Appliances and GE Plastics before joining GEBIC, then described the process—skill building, visioning, defining the mission, forming teams where, she noted, "everyone signed up." GEBIC team building stages, she said, followed the traditional phases: "Forming, Storming, Norming and Performing."

Steve McKinlay said he had postulated it would be simple to move as he did in the past year from a team environment at GE Lighting, to GEBIC, right? "Wrong," he said. "It wasn't easy."

The challenge for anyone making this kind of change, said Steve, was "to live through chaos." He noted that when his former component, GE Lighting, formed its National Customer Service Center, it decided to become team-oriented right from the start, and therefore was further along in the team-building process, whereas GEBIC was just beginning. "Everything at GEBIC was new to me: people, personalities, rules, barriers, objectives, you name it. GEBIC was trying to effect a major cultural change with a more senior work force that was already in place, and it was a shock to the system."

Some people at GEBIC, Steve said, couldn't or didn't want to adapt. "But it can work," he said. "And when it does, it's both satisfying and rewarding. Individuals who are adaptable will succeed and thrive."

Tom Lee, a 14-year GE veteran who came from the company's power generation business, then reiterated the gains in quality, cost and productivity that had been made. "These figures," he said, "should convince any doubting Thomases." With a smile, Tom admits that at the beginning of GEBIC's journey toward self-direction, he too was a doubting Thomas.

Tom stressed that "GEBIC has moved from being a 'Yes but'er' to a 'why not'er.' "And the reason why is summed up in three words: Caring. Sharing. And Trust."

Frank Doyle thanked the group—for what they had accomplished, and for the spirit in which they had accepted the challenge.

In reporting to their teammates back in Albany, the GEBIC presenters noted that some in the audience at Fairfield hardly reacted to their presentation. But Tom Lee spoke for the group when he said, "it's probably unfair to expect people to know what self-direction is all about in just one hour. You almost have to live through it to understand it."

The Doyle presentation is a perfect example of the self-confidence generated by empowerment, Susan Moyer believes. "We're like an island when you compare us with some areas of the company," she says. "They're organized like we used to be—a lot of formality with titles, positions and bureaucracy. In our old mode, you never would have seen us up there with Frank Doyle. Now, we go ahead and call on vice presidents when it's necessary to do our jobs. John doesn't worry; he has a lot of confidence in us."

This self-confidence makes Julie Dinardo feel that "I'm not just coming to work, but am part of something that's successful. I'm a part of the decision-making process. I like the feeling that I may work in a massive company, but I control a part of it.

"With this new way of doing things," says Julie, "you have to forget the past. That's particularly true of titles;

they become a necessary abstraction. Actually, in spite of the titles we carry, we're all managers because we're managing tasks and projects on our own. Once you get over that mental hurdle, you feel good about what you're doing. But to make the process work, you have to open your mind a crack."

Tom Lee agrees an open mind is crucial. "I'm flexible enough to get along almost anyplace. In fact, I thrived pretty well under the old system, and could put forth ideas. Whether management would consider them or not was another matter.

"Self-direction, however, adds a new dimension—the power of consensus. We've learned the power of working together as a team. Of course, there's that last piece you have to nail in place to make the structure complete—ownership. If people don't like something, they have to take it on and 'own' it until they find a solution."

Jacquie Braam believes this team spirit is at the heart of building self-confidence in GEBIC people. "Money from your pay and the bonus program is important, of course. But working as a unit is even more so. It makes you want to step forward and help others do the things that will move us up on the quality scale."

Frank Doyle ran into John Wilfore later in the year at a meeting in Chicago. He pulled John aside to again say what a great job he thought his people were doing, especially in regard to productivity.

Then he turned serious: "But you're making my estimates look bad. You told me going into 1991 that your operation would need 24 people to do its job. Now I find that you're doing it with only 21."

As Doyle started to return to the meeting, he winked and said, "John, I wish some of my other people were as lousy at estimating as you."

VII

Step Six:
Getting Out of the Way
■

If the essence of empowerment is to parcel out the traditional roles of management to the troops, then the question is: who needs a manager?

Richard Costello may have inadvertently seeded this cloud of doubt when he and John Wilfore were meeting one day with team members. As an aside, Costello noted, "GEBIC is moving from self-directed to self-managed."

In retrospect, John believes this casual comment—suggesting an organization without a leader—sparked a flame of panic in GEBIC. "I could almost hear our newer employees thinking, 'Great!' But the look on the faces of our longer-term people seemed to plead, 'My god, what are we going to do now?'"

Roz Wilkins says that she and others at GEBIC thought there was a conspiracy afoot to get rid of John. When Richard Costello heard of the repercussions from his compliment, he decided he'd better clear the air. So he traveled to Albany and told the people of GEBIC: "John Wilfore can stay here as long as he likes. John has no plans at this time to be moving on, and I have not given him that challenge."

Costello's comments banked the coals of rumor at GEBIC. But they didn't answer the basic question: when a self-directed work force is running full steam, does it really need a manager?

Or, in a more pragmatic vein: what's the manager's role with a self-directed work team?

After going through the process, John Wilfore is convinced the answer is clear-cut: to provide skills, knowledge and motivation. "A self-directed work team doesn't need a manager," he says. "But it does need a leader, who serves as a coach or a tie-breaker, to provide these factors. If the team doesn't get such a leader, then self-direction will never happen."

His people at GEBIC echo this view. And their observations provide grist for grinding out a new job description for him, if one should ever be called for.

First, they recognize that Wilfore handles a good many managerial and administrative duties that can't easily be delegated. As Jacquie Braam says, "he grapples with certain decisions— personnel, for example— that are beyond our current knowledge or skills." Wilfore says many of his people tell him the same thing. "They don't want to make the tough calls or the personnel decisions, and I don't blame them," he adds. "Sometimes they're not much fun."

It suits Rosalind Wilkins that Wilfore takes on those tasks. "I run a modeling business on my own time," she says, "so I have a feel for some of the problems he has to deal with. I suspect if we knew the things he confronts every day as a manager, we'd run the other way."

It makes sense, Wilfore says, to delegate to his people the jobs that can be delegated: "They know the operational details and problems better than I do."

John's people say they value his role for a second good reason— the expertise and guidance that comes from his long experience in business.

"People have great ideas," says Loretta Wilary, "and if they're recognized for them, they'll come up with more. Under the old system, we were never asked, or people were afraid to bring them up, or felt threatened by their manager. But not with John. He encourages us and offers his advice and counsel." And, she laughs, "he often does it in a round-about way by saying, 'I understand the problem. Now, what's your solution?' "

Cheri Lussier describes Wilfore's role as constructive. "He'll say, 'that's a good idea, but maybe you ought to look at it this way.' That helps keep us on track."

Debbie Krutz, a specialist in marketing information systems, who's on assignment at GEBIC from GE Corporate Information Technology, says this helps them gain a more complete picture. "He has us look at a problem from our own perspective."

By the nature of this guidance, Chris Berglund sees Wilfore as a "kind of father figure." And David Cairns reinforces this view. "He considers us grown-ups and professionals, and lets us do our jobs. But he's there if we need help, advice, or added resources."

Susan Moyer says, "if we don't agree with what he says, we tell him. He's made it clear we can take his advice or leave it." Nora Richter notes that, "of course, that has its drawbacks. More and more, he suggests we rely on our own expertise. He's not as much of a buffer for us as he used to be against outside influences. But as he says kiddingly, 'You brought it on yourselves.'"

Wilfore makes a third valuable contribution as an overseer or facilitator, according to Margi Call. "He's like the process observer Gary Martini told us about in our group dynamics sessions.

"Once GEBIC was delayered," says Margi, "John found he couldn't do the more traditional things GE managers have always done by themselves. He soon realized he *had* to delegate tasks to the troops and then trust us to get things done under his guidance. If not, he'd have been paralyzed, and so would we."

Evie DiDonato thinks this unbundling is the reason why Wilfore comes up with so many good ideas now. She feels it would be a shame "if he were still buried in instruction books and handbooks," the GE communications function he managed before coming to GEBIC.

Marie Murray visualizes Wilfore as one who's been named coach in a brand-new sport. "He's from a different time period, and has to learn a lot as he goes along."

What Wilfore learns, he tends to share openly, observes Debbie Krutz. "He goes beyond operational matters and actually solicits inputs on other business issues. He recently took time to include the staff in the budgeting process. That's unusual in GE. Money is usually the last thing a manager spreads out in the sun for everyone to see."

Paul Chmielewski is encouraged that Wilfore "shares the word" on self-direction and team accomplishments beyond GEBIC. "He's been our ambassador to talk about the process and our experiences throughout the U.S. and in both England and Europe. That's bound to be good for GE and for all of us at GEBIC," says Paul.

Not everyone aspires to Wilfore's role as manager of a self-directed work team. Kevin Vaughn, for one, notes "I don't know if I could sit back and do it . . . to be so open, and leave it to others to dictate what your role might be."

John can relax, according to Nora Richter. "We won't ever be 'the monkeys running the zoo.' But with his encouragement, we're running more and more of the shop."

Both Richard Costello and John Wilfore actively participate as full-fledged members of GEBIC teams. But in the beginning they felt their way carefully in fashioning their new roles.

Costello was determined to show his commitment from the first day. "So I felt my role should be to kick off the process and then get out of the way.

"Events were already taking place. But I thought if I were a part of it, it would be confusing. And, frankly," he notes ruefully, "I didn't fully understand what was going on. Almost before I knew it, the process whetted my appetite, and I wondered, 'Why can't I be a part of this?'"

Reality told Costello that he was two steps up in the GE management hierarchy, and therefore it would be extremely difficult to keep in touch with the ground floor action. "I concluded the only sensible thing for me to do was to provide resources and guidance, but avoid the day-to-day details.

"One challenge for both John and me," says Costello, "was not to interfere too much. When a manager opens his or her mouth, too many times people take what's said as a managerial decision that's cast in concrete. Sometimes I think the only safe way is to not say anything.

"Of course," he adds with a shake of his head, "that's not right either, so finding the right balance is the trick."

Costello recalls that the early days of the process posed a difficult time for John Wilfore, as GEBIC manager. The center had experienced a continuing increase in call volume and, as a result, work tensions were on the rise. In fact, some program directors had already left. What was exhilaration to some was anxiety to others.

"The GEBIC people blew right through most of the obstacles," says Costello. "You'd think they had started up a race car. One could almost hear the gears grinding, and the noise of the engine."

John Wilfore, for one, felt at times that the team had left him behind. "There wasn't much reciprocity in the process. It seemed mostly taking on their part, with not much giving back. They had some problem with me, and I didn't quite know what to do about it."

Finally, says John, "I asked Gary Martini: 'If things are going so well, why am I so frustrated?' And he told me, 'Why don't you ask them?' So I called a meeting and laid the issue on the table. The group said they'd mull it over. They soon came back with a proposal.

The group told Wilfore he wasn't the only one with a problem. Their concern: "We spend way too much time poking around to find the outer limits of authority, to see

---

Who Decides?

John decides: salary actions
personnel issues
discipline

Team decides: operations

We decide: staffing needs
budget issues
everything else

Decisions, decisions. Frustrations and misunderstandings quickly fade when GEBIC's manager meets with employees to seek answers to "Who does what?" and "How far can we go?"

how far we can go." Karen Malaczynski reported to John for the group: "We tried to make a list of what decisions you will make, which ones we can make, and those which we should make together. Now," suggested Karen, "we need to know the limits, the rules."

Wilfore refused to define boundaries that would bristle with "Keep Out" signs. But he did emphasize that some operational areas were still off-limits due to factors beyond his control— company policy, for example.

Together, the group began to understand that some issues called for "John" decisions— salary planning was one. Others prompted "team" decisions such as operational issues and vacations. And finally, some were designated "we" decisions— planning new services, staffing, and so on. The answer heard most often to "Who decides?" began with, "It depends."

Both GEBIC employees and GEBIC efficiency gained from the get-together, through improved understanding and the self-confidence that resulted from trust implanted during the process.

More important, those attending felt that the meeting was a turning point for John Wilfore. From that day, they saw him as even more of a team member than he had been in the past.

On their journey toward self-direction, all of the people of GEBIC were transformed in the process. But Wilfore, as manager of the GE Business Information Center, showed the force of change more sharply than the others.

"You could see it happen over time in John," says Julie Dinardo. "He had come out of the old GE, and when our team progressed to a certain point, he was forced to let us loose, and wave us off with a 'Go!' It must have been hard for him because after some 30 years or so with GE he still had a lot of excess baggage and was clinging to some of the old ways.

"I guess we really didn't stop and think what he was going through," continued Julie. "He must have felt troubled and confused because of the challenges he faced. First, they delayered GEBIC, and it was up to him to usher some colleagues out the door. Then, they told him to bring those remaining up to a certain level of self-direction, and he didn't know exactly how to do it.

"I tell you," said Julie, "I would not have wanted to be him in July of 1989. But I wouldn't mind now."

Rosalind Wilkins saw first-hand the change that occurred in John, through her previous role as his secretary. "I always had a lot of respect for him because of his intelligence. But he wasn't very people-oriented. John would often close his door to imply, 'I'm busy.' But his door's never closed now."

Brian Babe recalls that "John wasn't very expressive. So we never really knew where we stood with him. He usually didn't talk to employees unless there was a problem. He's changed to where I think he's probably the best choice they could make for that job.

"But," adds Brian, "I also think John wouldn't be around today if he hadn't changed."

John Wilfore was out of town on business for a full week in August 1991 when the employees of GEBIC decided as a follow-up to a budget planning session that they should hold a second visioning session to update their original sight-setting of February 1990. One priority target was to try and identify systems and resources they would need for the following year. In no way did they intend to circumvent John's role as "manager" and leader in self-direction. John was an active team member, like everyone else; he just happened to be unavailable at that particular time.

The team felt the best way to approach systems planning for 1992 was to re-visit their mission statement before making any decisions and recommendations for action. In their newly acquired, take-charge manner, they just went ahead and did it.

When GEBIC team members reviewed the original statement, they saw no reason to tinker with it. They had woven it laboriously out of both conflicting and complementary viewpoints a year and a half ago. Because they had unanimously approved it at the end of their deliberations, they now considered their mission firmly implanted. It had formed the constant banner toward which all of their efforts were focused.

Many of the major goals and tasks identified during the original revisioning and mission sessions had been targeted for completion in three to five years. Most of them, they now realized, had been completed in less than half that time. "The team was surprised they had accomplished so much from their list," comments Gary Martini. "They were not the only ones. That level of accomplishment has never happened before in my experience with other teams."

The people of GEBIC admired Gary for his previous involvement and contributions. This time around, they had considered asking Gary to help, but decided to go it alone.

As Richard Costello observed, "they felt they knew themselves better than any outside consultant. Also, they had not only learned the skills called for by the process, but were applying them. Then," added Costello, "Gary had almost achieved his objective; he had essentially worked himself out of a job."

On more than one occasion, Martini had told them: "You'll know it's working when you don't need me anymore."

New Goals from Revisioning

- Provide better information to customers

- Improve GEBIC skills and knowledge

- Manage appropriate growth of services

- Increase value of GEBIC to GE businesses

- Improve productivity and morale

Visioning revisited. GEBIC team members consider their mission an unchanging strategic beacon for action. But a year and a half after it was implemented, many of the long-range tasks have already been accomplished. Now, they feel it is time to rethink their tactics and consider new challenges. This is the result.

The revisioning session, according to Costello, moved the team into a brand new phase of the self-direction process. "It was apparent they had reached a higher level of skill development, team-building and maturity in both a business and personal sense. They were positioning themselves to tackle a whole new set of issues."

These evolved from a storyboarding session that kicked off revisioning. The days of petty gripes were diminishing. Instead, the GEBIC team came to grips with strategic insights relating to business and leadership issues.

Conduct at the revisioning session was brisk and to-the-point. GEBIC members reviewed the objectives of the meeting, heard team presentations (enforced by a strict limit of five to seven minutes for each), and began to search for ways to match issues with teams.

"We felt we were at a good comfort level," says Becky Raimo. "First, we wanted to identify new business objectives and opportunities. We also hoped the refocusing would tell us if our team constructs were still valid, or maybe we needed to reformat them — you know, kill some of the old teams, add new ones, whatever."

A new team did emerge along the way to revisioning — Internal Communications. It was spawned from the concept of the Easy Access team, which focused on external communications. The new team, they decided, should target internal communications: how is the process going, how do you feel about it, what are some of the issues facing us daily? Office morale and individual recognition were also tagged as prime targets.

Both the Sharing Knowledge and Accurate Answers teams had sensed from the beginning that they were linked by a mutual pursuit — training. So they merged, adopting tasks to resolve revisioning issues two and three: issue two — improve GEBIC skills and knowledge — would prepare the GEBIC team for expanded responsibilities; issue three — manage appropriate growth of services — would increase the strategic value of GEBIC to GE businesses.

The fourth GEBIC team, Rewards and Compensation, had by now successfully launched its bonus program. So it joined with the already functioning Internal Communications team to address such continuing issues as recognition and morale, and to promote GEBIC services. Members of the latter team realized, much to their chagrin, that at this late date they had neglected another "internal" part of the company— GEBIC itself. Toward that end, the new team adopted issue five — improve productivity and morale — and took on a new team name.

Members called themselves the "Musketeers," an acronym for the rewarding qualities they intended to nurture at GEBIC— *M*utual respect, gained through *U*nderstanding, *S*haring, *K*indness, *E*steem, *T*rust, *E*ncouragement, *E*nthusiasm, *R*ewards, and *S*atisfaction. The nickname cemented one more course on a rock-solid GE foundation — acronyms, which are sure to outlast any new form of organization GE people may create.

The revisioning session produced a potential new opportunity— the GEBIC Advisory Team, which focused on sharing of best practices. Members of this embryo team reasoned: why not go out and spread the word throughout GE on what GEBIC has been up to, on the assumption that others can benefit?

Sharing best practices. Facilitator training at GEBIC prompted Loretta Wilary (left) and Linda McClain to volunteer to help other GE businesses conduct Work-Out sessions. They are asked to meet with managers from throughout the company on a priority topic at GE: Health Care.

The team reported: "We're not trying to replace Gary Martini in such matters as skill building or group dynamics, where you need a consultant. We intend to explore areas where we have some expertise ... for example, empowerment, team-building, interviewing new hires, and measurements."

They sprinkled their enthusiasm with some self-interest, of course. It would be a good way to not only demonstrate but enhance GEBIC's team-building and empowerment. It could also elevate the skills and career path of participants.

The budding consultants concluded, however, that they should learn to walk before they ran — "sharing in a small team environment," as Tom Lee puts it. So members have been reaching out selectively.

Tom Lee, for example, made presentations at the GE Corporate Information Technology's megacenter in Schenectady and at GE's Corporate R & D Center in nearby Niskayuna. Becky Raimo did the same at GE Computer Services, and Steve McKinlay at GE Motors. And the advisory team provided the springboard for the Work-Out sessions conducted by Loretta Wilary and Linda McClain with GE corporate components.

There may be some pay-offs to GEBIC down the road. But participants see the activity now as dues for their membership in the GE club. Their presentations also feed fuel to Jack Welch's admonition that GE people share their best practices throughout the company.

When John Wilfore returned from his trip, the GEBIC team briefed him on what they'd been up to in revisioning — taking a new look at the mission, reviewing major business objectives, and the structure of teams needed to address those objectives. Once completed and documented, they resumed their activities. John didn't blink, and they didn't skip a beat.

Later, after John absorbed the full dimensions of their accomplishments, he complimented them and indicated his pleasure with the quality and quantity of their work. "You're at the top of my scale," he said. "10's all the way!"

Jacquie Braam recalls the revisioning session as a unique form of problem solving. "I missed the first visioning session," she says, "but I can't believe it was any better than this. Before coming to GEBIC, I was in one of GE's younger businesses and also in one of its oldest ones. I liked the people in both places, but nothing they did came close to what we're doing at GEBIC."

Along with improving their everyday work, the people of GEBIC, with John Wilfore's encouragement, are literally charting their own future. "I can't think of any other place where you can have such an impact on what your job will be in the future," notes Kevin Vaughn.

Steve McKinlay underscores that view. "The revisioning session worked so well because there was plenty of give and take. We were like a basketball team, with strong and weak points among the players. But nobody cared if they had to defer to a Michael Jordan as long as he scored 40 points."

Is there a painless way for an old-line manager to "get out of the way" so self-direction can work?

There's no patent formula and the process won't be painless, if John Wilfore's experience is any clue. But the comments of his people indicate that the rewards make the journey worthwhile for everyone.

Margi Call observes that "John Wilfore has made a real attempt to communicate everything, even though we might not like some of the messages or decisions. The other side of the coin is that he's the only one that has the 'altitude' to make some of those decisions. We're comfortable with that."

Becky Raimo seconds that feeling. "We understand if he tells us we can't do something or don't need to, because he tells us why. He manages when he has to. It's interesting working with John now. But it never would have happened if he hadn't been willing to change."

Julie Dinardo thinks it's fortunate that "John gives us feedback on everything. Without it, we might wind up in a psychiatric ward." Part of the reason for that feedback, she's convinced, is the support given by Costello and Frank Doyle. "I'm convinced they appreciate the difference between the way we were and the way we are now," she says.

It's apparent from John Wilfore's actions that he, too, discerns the old from the new, and has come to relish the difference.

"He's more than a manager," affirms Jacquie Braam. "He's a team player."

And, adds Evie DiDonato, "He approaches everything with total enthusiasm."

Perhaps Julie Dinardo sums up the transformation best: "We witnessed the deep struggle he went through. He's not the same person. He's a lot happier now."

VIII

Pebble in the Pond:
The Widening Impact

∎

Is GEBIC's journey toward self-direction for everyone? Not necessarily. But the documented record shows that it *can* be done and it *can* be successful.

Perhaps the most valuable contribution GEBIC can make for others is to raise the curtain of fear that cloaks the unknown.

There's no magic wand that waves everything into place. Each organization is different, and so are its people. But the basic principles that make the process work are firmly implanted along the way.

GEBIC's experience doesn't show what the result of the transformation will be for others. It only shows what happened for GEBIC. But it does show what can happen once an organization begins to build up a head of steam and gets under way.

The impact of the self-direction process on GEBIC can be measured in several ways.

One is real, but intangible. People who make the journey feel good about what they've accomplished. They like the fact that they've gotten to know each other better, that they've enhanced their individual contributions through team work, and that they've had a hand in deciding where they go, what they do, and what it means to them.

A visitor senses this feeling of well-being on entering GEBIC's lobby. One sees right away that this is not just another office, detached from reality. Team members have removed the hotel-room art that formerly hung from the walls and replaced it with bright brass letters which impart their intentions to the world.

"Our Mission," on the left, extends a first greeting, with the details spelled out in brief, crisp words. On the opposite wall, to the right, is a no-nonsense bid for action: "When you need more information from GE . . . " It's bolstered by dramatic photos of GE's 13 businesses.

A few feet down the hall, on the opposite wall, is the follow-up: "Our people can help!" above individual photos of the team members. These are not your usual ID shots. The people of GEBIC make eye contact in workaday poses, as if they really are anxious to step down and talk with you about any problem.

The remaking of GEBIC's main entrance is significant since it puts the focus on the key elements— the value of the business and its people. The display of good feeling and pride sets the tone for GEBIC and is important, of course. But there are more precise ways to measure what the people of GEBIC have done.

Our People Can Help. As a member of the Visitor Team, Program Director Carol Van Riper quickly puts a guest at ease in the lobby as she begins a tour of GEBIC. The demeanor of pride and helpfulness in GEBIC people is visually reinforced by the mission statement and photos of team members.

Some accomplishments come from the larger, more traditional factors — productivity and customer satisfaction. As noted earlier, both have rocketed beyond the norm for comparable service groups.

But the impact of these are shored up by tangible accomplishments that are not as readily apparent.

GEBIC in fact has made it easier for customers to do business with GE. A toll-free number offers easy access. Spanish-speaking team members with back-up in other languages extend a welcome beyond U.S. borders. Other GE people who are most likely to have trouble fielding customer calls now know that GEBIC can help.

GEBIC team members have made sure that callers get faster, more accurate answers. They've devised a sophisticated new computer system, along with "Playbook" software, for call handling. They've arranged, on their own, to do a better job of taking after-hours calls in their own homes, using cellular phones and laptop computers linked to GEBIC data. And they continue to extend and reinforce their contact network of GE expertise for special help.

Team members have not only propped up GEBIC's level of professionalism, they keep it up. They plan and conduct interviews for new hires, then develop and carry out mentoring, orientation and training programs.

They've enhanced the work environment at GEBIC — initiating weekly "dress down" days, acknowledging birthdays, moving the conference room to bring people together, solving the sticky problem of vacation scheduling by doing it themselves, even taking care of such pesky amenities as the periodic defrosting of a small refrigerator, maintaining a water cooler and filling the in-house soda machine.

And last — a major accomplishment in any business book — team GEBIC created and launched a bonus program that rewards people performance according to customer satisfaction.

Many of these tangible accomplishments were spontaneous by-products of the self-direction process. No one sat down and planned every one of them. Most times, team members saw to them as the result of common sense. They needed to be done.

The people of GEBIC are quick to note that the impact of self-direction brings risks along with the rewards.

One danger is the loss of individuality, according to Steve McKinlay. "Sometimes people feel they're more productive than others, and don't get the proper recognition. They just have to bite their tongues."

Carol Van Riper agrees. "You have to juggle the needs of the team with those of the individual, because all of us have needs. It's sometimes tough, though, to subvert your individual desires because GEBIC has some pretty strong individuals. There isn't a shrinking violet in the lot."

It takes a while to get used to this spirit of wide-open team play, according to Linda McClain. "Before," she says, "it was always *my* territory." Marie Murray senses that she's already lost some individuality. "But I try to keep in mind that what we're creating is bigger than the sum of the parts."

The pace of the self-direction process often becomes so intense that it threatens burn-out, Karen Malaczynski warns. "So I offered to leave my phone duties for a couple of hours a day and help the support staff maintain the database we all use. The change of scene made a big difference."

Kevin Vaughn observes the same challenge. "The team dynamics brings constant change, which is both good and bad. It's bad if you get caught up in the flurry and don't quite know what role to take. But when you catch on, there's a great sense of exhuberance."

The flurry carries with it the same conflicts that you find in any office, Linda McClain notes. "The difference is that we deal with them out in the open and, therefore, everyone knows about them. It's one of the trade-offs with the good features."

Mike Marchi doesn't believe his former co-workers realize the full impact of the gains they've made through self-directed teamwork.

"It's the blue spruce theory all over again. They say to me, 'Things are not much different than when you left.' But when I visit, I see more volume, more quality, more accomplishments, and more pride. The customer satisfaction scores alone prove the magnitude of what they've done, and how much they've changed."

Becky Raimo knows she's been transformed along with GEBIC. "I'm a different person when I'm here. Everything's open and honest and we're urged to say what we think. Away from the office, I tend to be more careful about what I say. People on the outside don't always *want* you to tell them everything."

"There is an openness that was totally lacking in my previous job," says John Madigan. At GEBIC, he relates, "your inputs are worth something because you're in the loop of the business. Also, you always have a good idea of how well you're doing because survey results are up there on charts in the hallway."

This open climate has stimulated an unusual flush of freedom, Kevin Vaughn believes. "It's another name for ownership. We've been given the chance to run the place the way we think it should be run." Marie Murray likens it to "being let out of a cell. Most jobs confine you to your own little area, and you don't dare try to learn something else. Now, I'm involved and people care about what I think."

That freedom transfers into positive career aspirations. David Cairns, who joined GEBIC less than a year ago from

Nurturing growth. The people of GEBIC have created a relaxed environment that encourages all to reach out to help each other learn and grow.

the outside, relishes the chance to work with people throughout the company. "It's a unique and wonderful opportunity to enhance my future," he says.

Skills attained in the self-direction process should help those who leave GE, says Nora Richter. "I was manager of an outside firm before coming to GE," she says. "I know they'll be valuable to anyone who gets the chance to run his or her own company."

The self-direction process is even linked to families, according to Steve McKinlay. But, he says, the bond can be tenuous. He recalls telling his brother and his father, a long-term GE employee, about Wilfore's intent to go from center manager to team leader. "My dad said, 'It'll never happen.' They just don't understand how the process works."

Rosalind Wilkins also notices that outsiders see the change in GEBIC's working environment. "A visitor poked his head in our kitchen the other day and remarked, 'This place looks great. Where do you work?' Then he added, half jokingly, 'It can't be GE!'"

The self-direction process has made a marked impact on GEBIC's manager, John Wilfore. "John's eyes light up when he talks about the people and the process," according to Julie Dinardo. "He feels very fortunate because not too many other GE managers have gone through it to this extent."

Serving as leader and coach of a self-directed work team is not without its trials. John Wilfore came face-to-face with a conventional challenge shortly after taking over as head of GEBIC: how to handle changes in the personnel make-up of the organization.

The previous policy at GEBIC called for hiring people with long GE experience. They brought with them a technical background, experience in several businesses and, of course, some relatively high salaries. They also lugged along, as one might expect, long tenure. "It was the old S-curve," Mike Marchi notes, "the thing that happens to people. They mature, level off, and then get stale when they're not challenged."

Wilfore decided to take a different tack. He and Richard Costello devised a "flow-through" strategy for staffing. It called for hiring people with lots of customer service and telephone experience plus people skills, but little or no GE experience. This brought an infusion of high potential and lower pay to GEBIC. But at the same time, it created a two-tiered salary structure.

In a traditional GE hierarchy, this would incite the troops to mutiny. Long-term people naturally want to protect their advantageous positions. Newer people, on the other hand, resent the disparity in pay and status. And it's compounded by the lack of opportunity to move up in a traditional organization, which tends to be static by nature.

While this might happen in a hierarchical business structure, it did nothing of the kind at GEBIC.

The reason: while not all the higher salaried people embrace the flow-through personnel concept with gusto, and some may even be uneasy about it, at least they're not in the dark. They know all about it, along with John's rationale. So do the younger people. There aren't many secrets at GEBIC.

The Flow-Through concept. John Wilfore briefs new Program Director Valerie McCormick on GEBIC's personnel philosophy, which emphasizes prior customer service experience and expanded company-wide opportunities for promotion.

The impact of Wilfore's strategy promises to invigorate everyone. As the textbooks say, it's Win-Win-Win, though making it happen in tough economic times is not easy.

Newer people at GEBIC like the flow-through philosophy because, since there are now fewer managerial spots in GEBIC, it opens the door to more rapid advancement elsewhere in a very large company. Those with more service stand to gain because it helps them bypass the roadblock of salary ceilings via a ticket to better jobs in other parts of GE.

The GE businesses who hire from GEBIC get people who are savvy about team-building, empowerment, and self-direction. Even if the businesses don't choose to head in that direction, they get skilled employees who are knowledgeable about themselves, the work environment, and GE. And, of course, the company wins every step of the way.

The outgoing involvement of GEBIC people in the everyday world of GE helps lubricate Wilfore's flow-through process. GEBIC consulting-type work is a good example. "It can be the carrot that gets them better jobs," says Mike Marchi.

"Consulting wasn't a factor in my going to GE Medical Systems," notes Mike. "But my GEBIC experience did break an old hiring mold at Med Systems. They had never hired anyone for my new job with a sales and marketing background."

Julie Dinardo is convinced her GEBIC experience "will be valuable the next place I go. I've learned more here in two years about facilitation and skill-building than I did in my previous 10 years."

Rosalind Wilkins found out first-hand what the impact of GEBIC's journey had been on Richard Costello. "When he visited us in mid-1991, I asked why he hadn't been up to see us lately. He told me, 'I used to feel your team needed direction, focus and guidance. Now, I don't feel I'm needed as much.' "

Costello is pleased that management demands have lessened because of self-direction. However, he reports the initial impact was greater than what one might expect from the old GE school of management. "The things you've always done, the things that come naturally — now, they're not always the things to do.

"I'll give you an example," Costello relates. "John Wilfore told me he wrote a letter to his people recently about a personnel decision that he considered trivial. It caused an immediate uproar because it wasn't trivial to the team. They needed to know why and how the decision was made. Several asked him: 'Why didn't you choose me?'

"It shows how important it is to urge your people to tell you if something is important to them. You have to be careful about what you do, and how you do it, and be as sensitive to employee feelings as to your own," he says. "The times when you think only of yourself are long gone."

Costello believes that more and more GE service operations are dipping their toes into the mainstream of self-direction or team-building, if the number of visitors to GEBIC is any guide. "If I were to start all over again, I'd do the same thing. But when we began, we couldn't find many practical role models.

"When you do find one," he says, "one of the first things you'll learn is that progress will be gradual because it *is* a learning process. In fact, it still is for GEBIC."

Julie Dinardo suspects that topside approbation is the reason GEBIC was invited to make the Doyle presentation. "After we left, I'd be surprised if he didn't urge all of his managers to give self-direction and empowerment a try, as Costello did. I don't know if any rose to the bait. If not," she says, "it could be that they didn't feel they needed it because their work was more task-oriented than people-oriented."

Most GE organizations sense the oncoming impact of empowerment and self-direction, whether they're into it yet or not, for a good reason: CEO Jack Welch is pushing it. One suspects that if he could, he'd wave a wand and jump-start the whole company in a giant whoosh. It would be the simple way to accomplish many of his stated goals.

The logic goes like this: The self-direction process brings empowerment. That lets employees, on their own, cut out the nonsense that's traditionally slowed down business, and find better ways of doing things. There's that GE (i.e., Welch) word for doing this: Work-Out.

Assuming that this gets the GE juices flowing freely, the next logical move is to spread the word. There's also a GE term for that: best practices. Welch has already expressed his view on the subject in, among other places, the Harvard Business Review: "Transfer best practices across all the businesses, with lightning speed."

Again, it seems to be happening, but not at lightning speed. And, it's not going to be easy. Old habits die hard.

GEBIC people talk to a good many others throughout GE whose organizations are involved in various kinds of team-building. Many of them, however, report that what's going on is not yet self-direction. Reports Julie Dinardo: "Some say their managers tell them how and when to breathe."

But some of the ancient bastions are crumbling.

Over a good many years, for example, GE favored pooled sales organizations as the way to bring to customers the wares of various GE product operations— via industrial sales, utility sales, component sales, and so on.

Back then, their customers were "indexed," which was another way of saying: "Keep away." Other GE people were not supposed to contact or talk to those customers and prospects without first checking with the assigned sales engineers.

Today, those sales groups see GEBIC as an ally, not an antagonist. GEBIC is a safety valve that let's them quickly and easily pass off misdirected customer calls, field arcane questions that used to bog down sales people, and— of great importance— re-direct the flood of incoming calls that should, for efficiency's sake, go to GE distributors.

"GEBIC lessens the load for a lot of us in sales," observes Eric Pomering, who is GE's Midwest Corporate Area Manager. "It's one of the few places inside GE that has a total company overview."

From the time GEBIC began its transformation, its best practices stemming from self-direction have dramatically improved— to lean on an early Jack Welch aphorism, they're growing "better than the best."

Customers served per GEBIC employee totaled 3,698 in 1989, the first year of the self-direction process. That number rose to 4,564 in 1990, took a huge leap to 6,038 in 1991, and will jump to about 6,600 in 1992.

John Wilfore says it's pretty obvious that GEBIC can't hope to maintain the trajectory of productivity on a steeply rising straight line. But the gains still promise to be impressive, even if they start leveling off. GEBIC's yearly gains over these four years have ranged from a high of 49% to a "low" of 19%.

Gary Martini, believes this progress is partly due to subtle factors that are more apparent to outsiders than to those within GE.

"For one thing," he says, "GEBIC is located away from traditional influences. Its people are in a building that's separate from GE plant operations in the area. Even their address— One Winners Circle— gives them a subconscious boost."

Management support provides another, he says. "Some managers *allow* the self-direction process to get under way. The people of GEBIC were encouraged to go for it by managers who are *champions* of the concept— Richard Costello in particular."

Martini also believes that GEBIC has created a climate that's unique in the top tier of Fortune 500 firms. "GEBIC acts with the speed and agility of a small company while being part of a large one," he says.

"That borders on the concept GE promoted a few years ago: dual GE citizenship. The idea was to act like an entrepreneur, with the confident knowledge that you had the resources of a technological leader to back you up when you needed help."

The most powerful influence, says Martini, "comes with the territory, GEBIC's reason for being: to keep in close, daily contact with the customer in a way that makes it easier for them to do business with GE."

Martini believes this contact also positions GEBIC to provide early warning on what's right or wrong with the company. It offers GE the same advantage that computer upstarts have over their well-entrenched but slower moving competitors.

One gains further insight into the impact that self-direction has made on GEBIC by asking a couple of questions. The first: would you want to go back?

Margi Call and Julie Dinardo reply as if in unison: "I can't imagine anyone wanting to go back to the old ways."

Mike Marchi reinforces their view, but with a twist: "You've got to be kidding. This is more fun."

A second question to the people of GEBIC: what's been your most memorable experience from the process?

Their responses indicate they enjoy the best of two worlds— freedom as individuals, and pride in their accomplishments as a part of the team that is GEBIC.

"I like the freedom of decision," says Chris Berglund, "of doing what you do best, with no one standing over your shoulder, telling you what to do." Deb Reutter agrees: "Everybody has ability. They just need a chance to show it."

Kevin Vaughn observes that "there's a great deal of satisfaction in coming to work every day because you're allowed to do your own job. But then, I think of what we did at the revisioning session and I just shake my head— there was no leader, no consultant . . . the team did everything."

The way team members reinforce each other is also memorable for Becky Raimo. "It confirms what we learned at the start— you need several kinds of people to be successful."

Cherie Lussier relishes the idea of being on a team. "It's a very good feeling that you can sit down and discuss issues and actually change things." Marie Murray also is grateful for "this whole idea of working together. I never had it in any other position at GE."

Several see sharing as their most vivid memory of the self-direction process. Paul Chmielewski, for one, affirms that "it's been an eye-opener to see the change while we went from individual *contributing* to individual *sharing*." Tom Lee calls it "the very essence of what we've talked about all through the process— sharing, caring, trust." And Evie DiDonato adds, "it's been wonderful to participate in the growth of the center . . . the whole process."

The most memorable experience for most GEBIC people has been the impact on their personal lives. David Cairns says, "it's taught me to deal with people on the outside I don't ordinarily deal with. I think serving customers has brought out the best in me."

Julie Dinardo believes "It can do great things not only for our jobs, but for our lives. It's been hard, but it's been worth it."

Margi Call knows it's been good for her. "It's given me the opportunity to choose my own growth area. When we first began the team-building process, I noticed that another person in operations, who had a 'full plate,' was carrying out functions that were of little interest to her, but were of great interest to me. I suggested that I take over the functions, and I wound up managing the work."

The self-direction experience changes the way people think about moving on, too, says Steve McKinlay. "Most of us want more responsibility, or maybe want to be a manager or team leader. But I'd find it difficult to leave this group, because I think it's the best team. It would be like going from the Lakers' basketball team to the Celtics. Not bad, but you'd carry along a lot of memories of the Lakers."

Jacquie Braam looks toward "the realization that one of my long-time dreams may come true— that we can work together, come together, and support each other as a cohesive community. We're not there yet, but we're drawing closer."

In a sense, Jacquie echoes the words of Jack Welch when he introduced Work-Out in 1989:

"We want 300,000 people with different career objectives, different family aspirations, different financial goals, to share directly in this company's vision, the information, the decision-making process, and the rewards. We want to build a more stimulating environment, a more creative environment, a freer work atmosphere, with incentives tied directly to what people do."

The Continuing Journey
■

Where does the GE Business Information Center stand in relation to other groups which are working toward self-direction?

GEBIC's manager, John Wilfore, says you can't compare GEBIC with others. "It's the nature of the process," he affirms. "Where you are is where you are."

A fuzzy answer? GEBIC's consultant, Gary Martini, says no, and reinforces Wilfore's view. "It depends," he says. "There are too many variables for a pat answer."

Both point out that the six-step process GEBIC undertook does not come with a map and clear directions. Therefore, once under way, you can't point to where you are.

Instead, the process is evolutionary, and different for every organization. Of course, it's natural for people to feel better if they know how far they've gone. But once a group has made progress and overcome obstacles, new obstacles will pop up. "That's why a manager can never say exactly where a group is at any one time," notes Wilfore.

The best course, according to Gary Martini, is to focus on the methods rather than just the accomplishments. He affirms that GEBIC has made the transformation to that level of understanding.

But even when people do accept this premise, says Wilfore, they still want to know: "How far can I go?" Again, Wilfore and Martini give the same answer: "It depends."

John explains: "For most people, this is a last tug on their security blanket. Back in the days of the 'old GE,' if you didn't know exactly where you were, you were considered lost. Now, in the 'new GE,' it's not that important. What *is* important is to answer the question: 'Where are you going?'

"If people want me to provide the answer, I tell them, 'you can go as far as you want to go.' At GE, I'd tack on one caveat, and I imagine it's appropriate at other companies: 'you can go as far as the system allows.' "

"That's no problem at GE," adds John. "Our CEO will cheer us on all the way. Jack Welch has stated he feels 'passionate' about energizing GE with Work-Out and, of course, self-direction is the embodiment of that concept."

John Wilfore recalls that Gary told them from the beginning that it would take a long time for GEBIC to become self-directed. But Martini also cautioned them not to think of it as a *long* journey.

Rather, he said, it would be a *continuing* journey.

Looking back, the GEBIC team recognizes the basic advancements that were made at each of the six steps in their self-direction process.

Step one— "Getting to Know You"— elevated members to the first level of understanding. "It taught us," says Mike Marchi, "that the first fix has to be the team and the peo-

---

The Journey to Self-Direction

Step One: Getting To Know You

Step Two: Setting Sights

Step Three: Sharpening Skills

Step Four: Taking Stock

Step Five: Unleashing the Power of Empowerment

Step Six: Getting Out of the Way

The six-step journey. A re-cap of the course taken by GEBIC as it evolved from a hierarchical GE organization to its present structure—a self-directed work team.

ple, not the business problem. Targeting the latter first will almost certainly stir up a new set of problems before you've developed the proper resources to solve the old ones."

Richard Costello likens the early part of the process to the parent-child relationship. "You remember the growing-up years: children wanting more, and you as a parent tending to give more. Eventually the children mature, and their values and perceptions change. Finally, both parents and children get to know each other better and build a closer, stronger relationship."

Costello sees GEBIC's intense "Getting to Know You" sessions as akin to the last stage of teen-agers. "At 17, they're convinced their parents don't know anything. Yet when they reach 20, they're amazed to find out how much their parents have learned in just three years.

"Those who attended the GEBIC sessions," says Costello, "were amazed to discover how much they'd learned in just a few hours. They found they were not only all *different*, but all *needed* in order to make team GEBIC whole. And successful."

People shouldn't worry if they get off to a rocky start on this first step, warns Gary Martini. "It's normal for any group to move ahead, fall back, then forge ahead again. That happens often throughout the process leading to self-direction."

Taking *Step Two—Setting Sights—* seemed intimidating at first to the people of GEBIC. But once they understood that their future actions were to be determined by a stated mission, as opposed to detailed plans, their pulses quickened.

Actually, GEBIC's mission had been ordained from the start: to make it easier for people to do business with GE when they didn't know who to call. GEBIC team members didn't quarrel with the purpose. They merely aimed it a notch higher. They strived for *satisfied* customers, with the degree to be determined by customers themselves on a *quality* scale.

"Quality results," they noted in an April 1991 report to GE management, is how "GE Corporate measures GEBIC." Also, they said, "it's a primary focus for General Electric in the '90s." And finally, they reported, it's "why we want to come to work every day!"

The fundamental advancement in step two, they found, was that self-direction by itself was not enough. To be successful, the team needed some *central* direction. With the mission providing a common, enduring beacon, team members could then apply their individual talents in creative ways to accomplish the mission.

In search of their own mission, the people of GEBIC discovered that the ones documented by entrepreneurially successful companies always focused on *people*— customers first, then people in the companies who served those customers . . . i.e., *all* employees.

"People are the key ingredient," says Kevin Vaughn. "And they need open and honest communications to make the process work."

In early December 1991, Frank Doyle reported to John Wilfore on a recent meeting he had attended with senior executives of Walmart, Conrail and GE Contract Sales. "They were all people-oriented," he said.

"You could almost visualize their formula for success as they talked," said Doyle. "From the first, it was clear they knew that the results of their companies were tied to their people. They put great trust in them, had a strong external focus, and were keenly oriented to action."

"That's a pretty potent formula for any business," he emphasized to John.

The challenge of *Step Three—Sharpening Skills*— was summed up recently by *Aviation Week*: "Hanging banners and giving employee pep talks, without making the fundamental changes required, only disillusions the work force and discredits the concept."

Gary Martini helped GEBIC's people make the needed fundamental changes— gaining new skills, such as how to run productive meetings, and how to solve knotty problems.

GEBIC's manager was not exempt from change either. As a team member, John Wilfore was expected to learn the same skills as his people. And as manager, he was faced with the added challenge of delayering.

Jack Welch had teed up the challenge: "When you take out layers, you change the exposure of the managers who remain. They sit right in the sun. Some of them blotch immediately; they can't stand the exposure of leadership."

Both John Wilfore and the other team members gained comfort in knowing that they now had learned the skills considered crucial to becoming a self-directed work force. But they heeded the caution of Gary Martini: their continuing focus should not be on the *tasks* alone, but on the *process*.

At *Step Four—Taking Stock—*the people of GEBIC paused to measure their progress, to see how well they had done, and to make sure their efforts would be adequately rewarded.

They concluded that the old standard measurement for GEBIC, volume of calls, did not focus enough on their mission. It did relate in an oblique way to their primary intent in serving customers—easy access and accurate answers. But it gave no good reading on one of their major goals—productivity.

So the people of GEBIC targeted the key yardsticks that would give them a good reading on productivity—customers served per employee, and the cost per customer served.

The team members rejected the suggestion that they should call in an outside consultant for help, and instead fashioned their own bonus program. Their initial guidelines stipulated that teamwork should override individual effort, the program should focus on meaningful business issues, and that rewards should be linked to customer measurement.

Documented results have shown that their formula has been hugely successful.

GEBIC team members had hardly left the starting gate for *Step Five—Unleashing the Power of Empowerment—*when they discovered a curious thing: individually, they were beginning to act more like managers than employees, controlling and directing their own activities as well as their own destiny.

They found that when they were handed the power to do things on their own, in the way they thought best, they automatically began to analyze obstacles, objectives, options, and consequences. Before, they had always expected their manager to take care of things like that. Now, it was up to them.

Most, but not all, relished the prospect. Those who did, flourished and learned from this new opportunity to direct their own affairs.

They were also surprised to learn that they had all become salespeople and marketers, no matter what their acknowledged duties. That outcome, they concluded, was inevitable because everything they did had to relate in some way to their mission: satisfying customers.

They also became as zealous as any hard-nosed GE manager about cost take-out. And why not? It was a natural outgrowth of finding easier and better ways to do things—Work-Out, if you will. Their rewards for doing so were directly linked to the doing, through their new bonus program, which they had crafted themselves.

One could almost surmise that the people of GEBIC had identified the last piece in the puzzle of perpetual motion—people.

"Anytime you put people in the equation though," says Chris Berglund, "you get the usual conflicts. But dealing openly with those conflicts strengthens the team, and it feeds on itself."

In any event, the people of GEBIC seem to have learned their lessons well. Gary Martini calls the level of expertise achieved by most GEBIC veterans "classic." They've acquired, he says, "all of the needed skills. John now has the philosophical requirements to do my work. And that goes for several of the others, too."

When GEBIC took *Step Six—Getting Out of the Way*—it was not a sidewater eddy that was soon to be swept away by the main GE current.

The company's Senior Vice President of Finance, Dennis D. Dammerman, reported in late 1991, "Within just a few years we will eliminate one-third of the managerial jobs at

GE. Not the people necessarily, but the titles, the titles that bring with them an implied mandate to control and to meddle."

Nor was it related to the rash of personnel cutbacks by other Fortune 500 companies in their tardy search for a competitive edge. GE sensed the coming onslaught from overseas a decade ago, and began to slim down to fighting trim. It is now three-quarters the size it once was, and is searching for ways to do more with its lean work force.

By what means? Again, Dammerman: "We have simply been astonished at the transformation that takes place in people in terms of productivity, creativity and receptivity to change when they are challenged, trusted, listened to and left alone."

The people of GEBIC, as one would expect, embraced the concept of self-direction. At the same time, they were sympathetic to John Wilfore's dilemma during the transition — the need to get out of the way.

To Wilfore — a traditional GE manager imprinted by years of conservatism — self-direction meant more of a change in mindset than habits. He was expected to transfer the powers of management to lower levels, make long-term commitments that led into the unknown, and rely on customer wants to magnetize the compass of GEBIC performance.

"John's problem," says Gary Martini, "was like that of any old-time GE manager. It was foreign to anything he had been used to. It was a challenge of *attitude*, not *technology*. That's tough for people who have been comfortable as linear thinkers."

Gary says he applauds the understanding and sympathy shown John by the others at GEBIC. "Managers like John are always under a lot of pressures. They're constantly being bombarded by problems of headcount, budget cuts, and so on.

"But once a manager makes peace with himself about self-direction — recognizing that employees can take a big load off the manager's shoulders, and can not only help get *more* things done, but help do them *better* — then the road to self-direction becomes easier."

Gary Martini believes that "the manager of the future really has no choice but to go the route of self-direction. 'Getting out of the way' is the proper strategy because all the options revolve around what the manager's people do."

Can GEBIC fit into the GE scheme of things? Or, put another way, can GE tolerate having a host of GEBIC-type clones conduct its business?

GE probably will have to if, like the rest of American industry, it wants to achieve one of its priority targets: productivity growth.

"The GEBIC model is not a panacea for all U.S. business," cautions Gary Martini. "The specs will vary according to the nature of a business and its problems." Again, he repeats, "it depends."

Carol Van Riper likely speaks for most GEBIC people when she reinforces that view: "Self-direction is not the perfect answer. It won't fit all businesses." And Kevin Vaughn concurs: "I've seen it from both ends—at one business where it didn't work, and here at GEBIC where it did. But I can also tell you I'm glad I'm here."

"A lot of people in GE want to go for self-direction," says Mike Marchi. "It's not very well understood. I think we'll see more and more of it in the company, but it'll be long term."

Will it be better for GE people?

"At GEBIC at least, we're better off and are trying hard to continue the growth," says Margi Call. "But the on-going struggles, the differences, the obstacles . . . they haven't all disappeared. It would be a mistake to think that we're 'fat and happy,' and nobody ever thinks about leaving."

"Maybe 'different' is a more appropriate word than 'better,'" says Loretta Wilary. "Sometimes I feel we're in a state of confusion. But it's good confusion, and I'd find it difficult to leave. We make things happen. It's never boring."

"Out there," Loretta says, waving to the outside world, "there are functional jobs. You go from here to there. That's tedious. At GEBIC, I enjoy it because things are always changing. Our jobs are never completely done."

How good a guide can GEBIC be to others?

Says Tom Lee: "Before, we were always trying to drive projects that somebody else told us to. Now, we're directed by the realities of the marketplace. A lot of people don't know how to do this, and I wouldn't say we're experts. We're learning, but we've only scratched the surface."

Richard Costello confirms this. "The self-direction process really is a continuing journey. There is no final destination. We've made progress, but now we're facing a whole new generation of issues, improvements that we hope will make our team even more self-directed.

"Everything hasn't been rosy in the past, and it won't be in the future. You get the bad along with the good.

"We don't have all the answers," Costello concludes. "But we're willing to share what we've learned with others."

Letting Go:
Lessons Learned

What are the important lessons learned at GEBIC that will benefit anyone interested in forming a high-involvement, self-directed work team?

The first and most important is that the process works, even in the service area where success stories are hard to come by. The verdict proclaimed for GEBIC by Richard Costello is clear-cut: productivity and quality are up, while costs are down.

Another is cautionary: don't expect miracles overnight. GEBIC's consultant, Gary Martini, says you should be prepared to meet three conditions before stepping out on your journey toward self-direction.

"First, you must understand that success won't come quickly— it will be a long-term process. Second, the managers must understand that the process does not happen *to* people but *with* people. And last, you don't have to understand the *how* of the process, but it's fundamental that you understand the *philosophy* behind it."

And what are the key ingredients of that philosophy? For the answer, one can turn to no higher authority than the members of Team GEBIC.

They have identified the following common elements as critical factors, although the emphasis may vary due to differing business conditions.

1. *Focus on people.* "Getting to know you" reveals the unique qualities of individuals. With understanding comes an appreciation of how each complements the others. Empowerment then instills individuals with the confidence and freedom to effect change . . . to weed out the old and introduce the new. This

can make all the difference between employee frustration and employee fruition.

2. *Create a team spirit.* Focusing on the team as well as the individual ensures that both will succeed. The manager no longer manages, but becomes a coach and a leader. "Give" and "Take" come in balance, while "we" replaces "I" as the most important word in the process. The priceless byproduct is support from one another, fueling the team with new vigor and strength.

3. *Build a caring, sharing environment of trust.* The first essential is an open mind, by all people at all levels. Ideas and needs gain a friendly reception, reinforced by concern and respect. Views are volunteered, not forced, and receive an honest hearing. In return, participants benefit from the cross-sharing of experiences and the nurture of insights that otherwise might never come to light.

4. *Provide focus and direction.* Step-by-step planning is edged aside by the standard of self-direction—the *mission.* It guides the efforts of individuals and teams toward their objectives, goals and tasks. One need no longer be paranoid about accomplishments, to the exclusion of almost everything else. In a free and caring environment, accomplishments will follow as surely as the night the day.

5. *Take your time.* Don't expect too much, too fast. The journey toward self-direction generates conflicts and setbacks. It's normal to fall back, then inch ahead again . . . to feel uncomfortable before feeling comfortable. Every so often stop, look back and recalibrate. Take whatever time is needed to do it right. It may not be easy, and it won't be overnight. But it will be worth it.

6. *Get management support.* Management has to believe in and be a part of the process. Pitching in at the grass roots level leads to understanding and a heartfelt commitment. And, only management can bring the air cover and resources needed for success: getaway meeting sites, advanced business systems

and most important, outside experts who can speed and smooth the way.

7. *Cultivate growth.* The self-direction process needs repeated applications of skill-building to flower into job satisfaction. But for participants, just "doing the job" is not enough; they must be given the opportunity to learn and grow and develop. In doing so, they will find ways to do things better. In reality, the resulting growth will produce dual satisfaction — in one's private life and in one's work life.

8. *Take meaningful measurements.* Along the way, participants need to know where they are and how they're doing. Honest, constructive one-on-one sessions between leader and individuals gauge progress, readjust targets and recharge motivational batteries. Periodic readings of team efforts — both qualitative and quantitative — help keep actions focused on the mission, and in particular at GEBIC on customer satisfaction.

9. *Reward what's important.* Focus on actions that are crucial to the mission. Then, link compensation to desired performance. As progress is made and rewarded, keep raising the bar height for both the team and individuals to create continuous improvement.

10. *Enjoy the journey.* It's an on-going process that daily offers new challenges and new delights. GEBIC people advise: "Don't rush it." "Take as long as it takes." "Keep it fun."

And, finally: "It's a lot of work, so be sure to laugh often."

WHO'S WHO
The cast of characters in "Letting Go"
■

The People of GEBIC: Three quarters of the members are program directors, handling incoming calls from GE customers and prospects. The others provide operational support for market applications, customer service, office administration, and data and communications. *Place of business*: One Winners Circle, Albany, NY 12205. 1-800-626-2004.

John F. Wilfore: Is Manager of the GE Business Information Center. He was a member of the original start-up task force for the center in 1984, following two decades of GE service in marketing, sales and computer-related work. *Place of business*: Same.

Richard A. Costello: Is Manager—GE Corporate Marketing Communications, a component of GE's External and Industrial Relations. He is responsible for all aspects of the company's communications with customers, its brand advertising, and the use of the GE brand image ("We bring good things to life"). The people of GEBIC report to him. *Place of business*: 3135 Easton Turnpike, Fairfield, CT 06431. (203) 373-2211.

Gary L. Martini: Is owner of Martini & Associates, Human Resource Consultants. The group specializes in organization and executive development, team building and training. *Place of business*: 17490 83rd Avenue North, Maple Grove, Minnesota 55369. (612) 574-6063.

James R. Burnside: The author is head of Corporate Communications, which specializes in business-to-business strategy, plans and execution; and the High Peaks Press, publisher of business and outdoor recreational books. *Place of business*: 2307 Cayuga Rd., Schenectady, NY 12309. (518)372-2605.

CREDITS

■

Foreword

Pg. x
- *The great equalizer*: Stephen S. Roach of Morgan Stanley & Co. New York, "Services Under Siege—The Restructuring Imperative," *Harvard Business Review*, September-October 1991, pg. 82.
- *GE productivity*: "A Decade of Opportunity," Dennis D. Dammerman, GE Senior Vice President, Finance, address to National Association of Black Accountants, June 28, 1991.
- *"Corporate Gullivers"*: John F. Welch, Jr., GE Chairman, "GE Keeps Those Ideas Coming," *Fortune*, August 12, 1991, pg. 41.

Chapter I

Pg. 4
- *"Strategic Intent"*: Gary Hamel and C. K. Prahalad, *Harvard Business Review*, May-June 1989, pg. 63.

Pg. 5
- *"Thriving on Chaos,"* Tom Peters, Alfred A. Knopf, Inc., 1987.

Chapter II

Pg. 7
- *Woody Allen*: Quoted in *The Wall Street Journal*, October 31, 1991, Pg. 1.

Pg. 10
- *Work teams*: Bibliography, from "Self-Directed Work Teams, The New American Challenge," Orsburn, Moran, Musselwhite and Zenger, *Business One Irwin*, 1990, pg. 332.

Pg. 14
- *LIFO*®: *"The Name of The Game,"* Dr. Stuart Atkins, *Ellis & Stewart*, 1981.

Chapter III

Pg. 19   — *"Speed, Simplicity, Self-Confidence"*: Noel Tichy and Ram Charan, *Harvard Business Review*, September-October 1989, pg. 120.

Pg. 20   — Ibid, pg. 115.

Pg. 21   — Ibid, pg. 113.

         — *Strategic Visioning*: Copyright by Gary Martini of Martini & Associates, Minneapolis.

Chapter IV

Pg. 33   — *Customer Experience Mapping*: Trade Mark of William J. Diffley of Diffley Associates, Madison, CT.

         — *"Speed, Simplicity, Self-Confidence"*: Ibid, pg. 118.

         — *Paradigms: TIME* magazine, January 14, 1991, pg. 65.

Pg. 34   — *"Discovering the Future . . . the Business of Paradigms"*: by Joel Barker. Copyright by Charthouse International, Burnsville, MN, distributed by Films, Inc., Chicago, IL.

         — *IBM: The New York Times*, September 15, 1991, Business section, pg. 10.

Pg. 43   — *Calibration-Team Building*: Copyright by Gary Martini of Martini & Associates, Minneapolis.

Chapter V

Pp. 48   — *Dell: The New York Times*, December 1, 1991, Business section, pg. 8.

Chapter VI

Pg. 59   — *The "egoless corporation"*: Alan Webber, editorial director of the *Harvard Business Review*, quoted in *Fortune*, October 7, 1991, pg. 48.

Pg. 59   — *"America's 100 Fastest Rising Companies"*: Ibid.

         — *"Speed, Simplicity, Self-Confidence"*: *Harvard Business Review*, September-October, 1989, pg. 116.

Chapter VIII

Pg. 95   — *Work-Out*: Ibid, pg. 116.

Chapter IX

Pg. 99   — *Fundamental changes*: Editorial in *Aviation Week*, December 9, 1991, pg. 7.

Pg. 100   — *"Speed, Simplicity, Self-confidence"*: *Harvard Business Review*, September-October 1989, pg. 116.

Pg. 101-102   — *Getting Out of the Way*: "A Decade of Opportunity," Dennis D. Dammerman, GE Senior Vice President, Finance, address to National Association of Black Accountants, June 28, 1991.